THE WORKING LIFE

A Roman Gladiator

Titles in The Working Life series include:

An Actor on the Elizabethan Stage

The Cavalry During the Civil War

A Colonial Craftsman

A Colonial Farmer

A Renaissance Painter's Studio

A Sweatshop During the Industrial Revolution

THE WORKING LIFE

A Roman Gladiator

DON NARDO

LUCENT
BOOKS ®

THOMSON
---*---™
GALE

San Diego • Detroit • New York • San Francisco • Cleveland • New Haven, Conn. • Waterville, Maine • London • Munich

© 2004 by Lucent Books. Lucent Books is an imprint of The Gale Group, Inc.,
a division of Thomson Learning, Inc.

Lucent Books® and Thomson Learning™ are trademarks used herein under license.

For more information, contact
Lucent Books
27500 Drake Rd.
Farmington Hills, MI 48331-3535
Or you can visit our Internet site at http://www.gale.com

LIBRARY OF CONGRESS CATALOGING-IN-PUBLICATION DATA

Nardo, Don,1947–
    A Roman Gladiator / by Don Nardo
      p.cm.— (The Working Life)
Summary: Discusses aspects of the life of the working life of a Roman gladiator, including
recruitment, training, weapons, and tactics,as well as how gladiatorial conflicts reflect
the values of their day.
Includes biographical references and index.
    ISBN 1-59018-480-7
    1. Gladiators- Juvenile literature. [1. Gladiators. 2. Rome—History—Republic, 265–30
B.C.—Empire,29 B.C.–450 A.D.] 1.Title. II. Series.

Printed in the United States of America

CONTENTS

FOREWORD

"The strongest bond of human sympathy outside the family relations should be one uniting all working people of all nations and tongues and kindreds."
Abraham Lincoln, 1864

Work is a common activity in which almost all people engage. It is probably the most universal of human experiences. As Henry Ford, inventor of the Model T said, "There will never be a system invented which will do away with the necessity of work." For many people, work takes up most of their day. They spend more time with their coworkers than with family and friends. And the common goals people pursue on the job may be among the first thoughts that they have in the morning, and the last that they may have at night.

While the idea of work is universal, the way it is done and who performs it vary considerably throughout history. The story of work is inextricably tied to the history of technology, the history of culture, and the history of gender and race. When the typewriter was invented, for example, it was considered the exclusive domain of men who worked as secretaries. As women workers became more accepted, the secretarial role was gradually filled by women. Finally, with the invention of the computer, the modern secretary spends little time actually typing correspondence. Files are delivered via computer, and more time is spent on other tasks than the manual typing of correspondence and business.

This is just one example of how work brings together technology, gender, and culture. Another example is the American plantation slave. The harvesting of cotton was initially so cumbersome and time consuming that even with slaves its profitability was doubtful. With the invention of the cotton gin, however, efficiency improved, and slavery became a viable agricultural tool. It also became a southern tradition and institution, enough that the South was willing to go to war to preserve it.

The books in Lucent's Working Life series strive to show the intermingling of work, and its reflection in culture, technology, race, and gender. Indeed, history viewed through the perspective of the average worker is both enlightening and fascinating. Take the history of the typewriter, mentioned above. Readers today have access to more technology than any of their historical counterparts, and, in fact, though they would find the typewriter's keyboard familiar, they would find using it a bore. Finding out that people spent their days sitting over that machine (with no talk of carpal tunnel syndrome!) and were valued if they made no typing errors because corrections were cumbersome to make and, in some legal professions, made documents invalid, is an interesting story that involves many different aspects of history.

The desire to work is almost innate. As German socialist Ferdinand Lassalle said in the 1850s, "Workingmen we all are so far as we have the desire to make ourselves useful to human society in any way whatever." Yet each historical period offers a million different stories of the history of each job and how it was performed. And that history is the history of human society.

Each book in the Working Life series strives to tell the tale of these anonymous workers. Primary source quotes offer veracity and immediacy to each volume, letting the workers themselves tell their stories. In addition, thorough bibliographies tell students where they can find out more information, and complete indexes allow for easy perusal of the text. While students learn about the work of years gone by, they gain empathy for those who toil and, perhaps, a universal pride in taking up the work that will someday be theirs.

THE ORIGINS OF THE GLADIATORIAL PROFESSION

The profession of the Roman gladiator was like no other in history. In fact, it would probably be more accurate to call it the "work" of the gladiator. This is because the word "profession" usually denotes a chosen line of work as well as one in which the worker receives regular compensation. However, most gladiators did not receive salaries (although winners of matches sometimes collected prize money). More importantly, they did not choose their line of work. The vast majority, including the lower-level gladiators who fought animals instead of humans, were slaves, criminals, or war captives who were forced to fight in the arena. (The arena was the dirt-covered, usually oval-shaped area where the matches took place.) A few were free individuals who volunteered. But once they had signed up, their status reverted to that of slaves; and along with slaves, prostitutes, actors, and other characters widely viewed as disreputable, they were branded with *infamia*, or a "bad reputation." Therefore, as noted classical scholar Michael Grant puts it, the gladiatorial ranks were "a refuge for social outcasts." [1]

This does not mean that crowds did not cheer gladiators, especially ones who won often. Indeed, some of the most successful fighters became leading sports figures with loyal fan followings and at times even groupies ready to offer them sexual favors. Such adoration existed only within the context of the events of the arena, however. No decent Roman woman would think of appearing at public functions with a gladiator, much less of marrying him. Gladiators were so reviled that even their lifeless bodies were denied entrance into cemeteries. Thus, the Romans had a marked and curious double standard when it came to gladiators.

MORTAL COMBAT IN FUNERAL RITUALS

The deep-seated mixture of disdain and fascination that Roman society held for gladiators may have been based on the gladiators' original servile role. Long before their combats were seen as a profession or even as work, the fighters themselves were viewed as things and property to be disposed of at will by their "betters." In Rome's earliest centuries, when an important man died, his family members, usually his sons, thought it their duty to appease the spirits of the dead. One way to do this was by offering a blood sacrifice in honor of the deceased. This was the origin of the Latin word for gladiatorial combats—*munera* (singular is *munus*), meaning "duties" or "offerings" to the dead.

At first, the sacrifice consisted of slitting the throat of a slave or a war prisoner on or near the tomb. Over time, however, the custom became more involved. Two slaves or prisoners were given weapons and forced to fight each other to the death, which spilled even more blood and, it was hoped, further satisfied the spirits. The audiences for these early funeral contests consisted strictly of mourners and invited guests; the public was not allowed to watch.

These early funeral combats appear to have originated in Campania, the fertile region surrounding what is now

Pairs of gladiators fight in this fresco (a painting done on wet plaster) created in the third century B.C. *in Campania, the region where such bouts originated.*

called the Bay of Naples, on Italy's southwestern coast. Paintings from the area dating to the fourth century B.C. show scenes from local funeral games, including contests such as chariot races, boxing matches, and fights between pairs of heavily armed warriors. That these fights were staged rituals rather than actual warfare is revealed by the presence of referees overseeing the combatants.

An important ancient written source also identifies Campania as the birthplace of Roman gladiatorial bouts. The long history of Rome penned by the first-century B.C. historian Livy discusses the connection between the first of many gladiator types, the "Samnite," and the Italian people for which it was named. Members of a group of hardy hill tribes, the Samnites were long rivals of Rome. They invaded Campania and occupied the town of Neapolis (Naples) before the Romans finally defeated them. After their win, the Romans held a large triumph (victory parade) to show off the prisoners and weapons they had captured. "By far the greatest sight in the procession," Livy writes,

> was the captured armor, and so magnificent were the pieces considered that the gilded shields were distributed amongst the owners of [Rome's] silversmiths' shops. . . . While the Romans made use of this armor to honor the gods, the Campanians, out of contempt and

hatred towards the Samnites, made the gladiators who performed at their banquets wear it, and they then called them "Samnites."[2]

INCREASINGLY BIGGER SPECTACLES

Eventually, the staging of gladiatorial fights at noblemen's funerals spread beyond Campania and by 264 B.C. reached Rome. That year two young men, Marcus and Decimus Brutus Pera, honored their father's memory by having three pairs of warriors fight to the death at his funeral games. Such combats quickly became popular, and in the years that followed more and more fighters took part. In 200 B.C. twenty-five pairs of gladiators fought at the funeral of the nobleman Marcus Valerius Laevinus; and in 174 B.C. thirty-four pairs grappled to honor the memory of the war hero Titus Quinctius Flamininus.

At this point, gladiatorial combats were still far from being a profession. The fighters received no formal training. And the bouts were staged informally wherever it was most convenient, most often in town squares and marketplaces. In time, seats were provided for the onlookers. Not long afterward, makeshift wooden structures began to be built so that the seats could be placed on risers, giving all the spectators a clear view of the fighters.

Steadily, as the spectacle of the combats became bigger and bigger, the fu-

A nineteenth-century engraving shows early gladiatorial bouts at a Roman funeral. In time, these fights became large-scale public events.

neral ritual aspect became less and less significant. At the same time, members of the public increasingly demanded that they be allowed to attend the fights. In this way, the once private and informal *munera* intended to honor the dead were transformed into public displays that people viewed as entertainment. By the first century B.C., gladiatorial bouts and fights between men and wild beasts were eagerly awaited public events in the Roman capital.

THE TRAGEDY OF THE GLADIATOR

This was the century in which the work of gladiators finally took on the trappings of what might be called a profession. The biggest single influence in this regard came from Julius Caesar (who would later win renown as a military general but who was at the time an aedile, an official in charge of maintaining public buildings and games). In 65 B.C. he staged the largest *munus* yet.

The event included 320 pairs of gladiators, which Caesar's political rivals feared he might use to take over the government. According to the first-century A.D. Roman historian Suetonius, Caesar

> collected so immense a troop of combatants that his terrified political opponents rushed a bill through the [legislature], limiting the number of gladiators that anyone might keep in Rome; consequently far fewer pairs fought than had been advertised.[3]

Caesar also wanted to give the state more control over these fighters and their combats, which before his time had been privately funded and run. To this end, he established a gladiator school (*ludus*) run by senators and other high-ranking Romans. Other similar schools soon opened, including one that trained those arena fighters who specialized in fighting animals.

Under such conditions, gladiators came to be seen as professional fighters. And at least from the perspective of their combat skills in the arena, they commanded a degree of respect. They could never attain the social status of Rome's true professional warriors—its soldiers—however. Therein lies the double standard and ultimate tragedy of the gladiator in Roman society. The audience admired the arena fighter for striving valiantly to imitate the soldiers who will-

A drawing shows the layered structure of a Roman amphitheater, including the awning that shaded spectators from the sun.

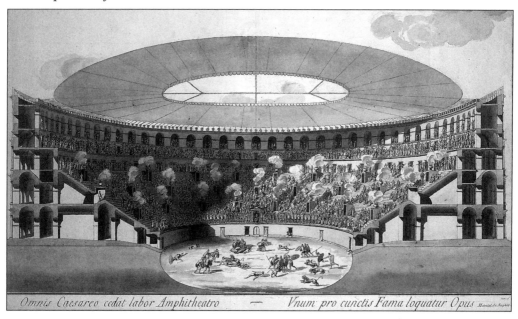

Omnis Caesareo cedat labor Amphitheatro — Vnum pro cunctis Fama loquatur Opus Martial.de Amphit

ingly risked their lives in battle for the fatherland; yet those same spectators looked on the gladiator as a debased, almost less-than-human thing worthy only of dying for their entertainment. As University of Massachusetts scholar Carlin A. Barton puts it:

> The gladiator's existence offered a form of simplified . . . soldiering, a means of gaining honor within a dishonorable situation and a way of transforming one's humiliation into a pattern of self-sacrifice. . . . It was clear to the gladiator . . . that those who would give him honor and glory were the very ones who despised him and who would take positive pleasure in his pain and death. [4]

Thus, the working life of a Roman gladiator might occasionally feature moments of public adulation and glory. But for the vast majority of these fighters, any such satisfying moments were heavily overshadowed by the shame of servitude and social rejection, not to mention the high likelihood of sudden, violent death.

CHAPTER 1

HOW PEOPLE BECAME ARENA FIGHTERS

The men, and on occasion women, whose work consisted of fighting in Rome's public games were of two general types. Some were gladiators, who fought one another. Their name came from the word *gladius,* which was a thrusting sword many of them used. It was also the standard sword used by Roman soldiers. The other general group of arena fighters were those who grappled with animals. Not as well trained as regular gladiators, the animal fighters were often viewed as less formidable, in a way the junior varsity of the gladiatorial world. Whether they were high- or low-status warriors, all had one thing in common. Namely, each spilled blood in front of cheering crowds, which made him or her something strange and disturbing to modern eyes—a combination of professional killer and professional entertainer.

Today, few people would willingly choose such a profession. And the same was true in the ancient Roman world. Most gladiators and other arena fighters were slaves, criminals, or war captives and had no choice but to train in gladiator schools when their masters or the state decreed it. Only a small minority of those who attended these schools started out as free individuals who actually volunteered to enter the bloody arena.

VOLUNTEERING FOR THE PROFESSION

Who were these volunteers? And why, in order to fight in the public games, would they willingly accept a demotion in their legal status to that of a slave, the lowest place in Roman society? Most volunteers came from the lower classes. Probably a majority were freedmen, former slaves who had earned their freedom. The sad fact was that society looked on freedmen as only slightly better than slaves. And freedmen had little opportunity for social advancement. So those ex-slaves who chose the arena and a return to slave status likely felt they did not have all that much to lose.

However, a few members of the upper classes volunteered as well, and they had much more to lose by sinking to the level of the gladiator. There had to have been some strong allure or concrete advantages to volunteering for the arena, no matter what class of free individuals one belonged to. "For one

GREEK INFLUENCE ON EARLY ROMAN FUNERAL RITUALS

One of the strongest influences on the Romans in adopting the custom of having warriors fight at funerals was the *Iliad,* a Greek epic poem dealing with the legendary Trojan War. Composed by the eighth-century B.C. bard Homer, the *Iliad* contains a vivid example of early Greek funeral rituals performed for great warriors who had died in battle. When the Greek hero Patroclus is killed by a Trojan prince, Patroclus's friend Achilles (the central character of the poem) sacrifices twelve Trojan children at the dead man's tomb. Then the Greeks hold athletic games in Patroclus's honor. In one of the events, two Greek warriors, Ajax and Diomedes, clash in single combat with swords and shields. The Romans were heavily influenced by Greek culture, including the characters and ideas of the *Iliad.* And these likely inspired or reinforced the custom of staging gladiatorial combats at funerals.

A chariot race highlights the funeral games of Patroclus, described in Homer's Iliad.

thing," historian Alan Baker points out, gladiators were renowned

> for their courage, morale, and absolute loyalty to their master. The martial discipline they maintained also meant that they received a level of respect and honor otherwise reserved for the Roman army itself. For some citizens, the choice to enroll in a gladiator school was made purely as a result of economic factors. Some were aristocrats who had squandered their inherited wealth and found themselves without the means to make a decent living. As gladiators, they would get three square meals a day, good medical care, and the opportunity to win money . . . for appearing in the arena. If they managed to survive long enough, they would eventually be granted their freedom. [5]

These same benefits appealed to many poor freedmen who had encountered difficulties in making a regular living since gaining their freedom. Some of the most desperate likely felt they faced a choice between a life of crime and taking their chances in the arena. If they could manage to avoid being killed or seriously injured while fighting gladiators or wild beasts, they had at least a shot at gaining a measure of fame and wealth.

Other reasons for volunteering for the arena were less practical and motivated more by thrill or pleasure seeking. There was the challenge and appeal of danger, for example, of living on the edge, as many race-car drivers and sky-divers do today. Still other arena volunteers hoped they would become popular idols and sex symbols who could have their pick of pretty young girls (or boys). That gladiators often became sex symbols, like some modern actors, athletes, and rock stars, is attested by a number of ancient inscriptions (words painted onto or carved into stone). Some were found in the ruins of Pompeii, a small Roman city buried and preserved by the ashfall from a volcanic eruption in A.D. 79. One Pompeiian inscription reads, "Caladus, the Thracian, makes all the girls sigh." Another declares, "Crescens, the net fighter, holds the hearts of all the girls." [6]

For the most part, these "girls" mentioned in the inscriptions were members of the poorer classes; it was considered unseemly for well-to-do young women to make public displays of any kind, much less fuss over low-life characters like gladiators. On occasion, however, the sexual attention that arena fighters attracted came from upper-class women, who always endured the rigors of shame and scandal as a result. In one of his satires, works widely read by Romans of all walks of life, the first-century A.D. humorist Juvenal lashes out at Eppia, a noblewoman who had the gall to fall in love with and run off with a gladiator. "That senator's wife,

A nineteenth-century painting shows women crowding around a gladiator who has slain his opponent at a private banquet.

Eppia, eloped with her fancy swordsman," Juvenal begins.

Husband, family, sister, all were jettisoned [abandoned], [with] not one single thought for her country; shamelessly she forsook her tearful children. . . . What was the youthful charm that so fired our senator's wife? What hooked her? What did Eppia see in him to make her put up with being labeled "The Gladiatress"? Her darling, her Sergius, was no chicken [youngster], [but was] forty at least, with a dud arm that held promise of [his] early retirement. Besides, his face looked like a proper mess, helmet-scarred, a great zit on his nose, [and] an unpleasant discharge from one constantly weeping eye. What

of it? *He was a gladiator.* . . . This is what she preferred to her children and her country.[7]

RECRUITING THE UNFREE

Juvenal did not say whether Eppia's lover, Sergius, originally volunteered for the gladiatorial ranks. If he did, he and others like him probably made up little more than 10 percent of all arena fighters. The bulk were unfree when they entered the profession and therefore were unwilling recruits.

The sources of these servile recruits were many and varied. And someone had to seek out and collect them in one place so that they could be either rented or sold to the people who ran the public games. Before the mid–first century B.C., the primary collectors of recruits

Oliver Reed (left foreground) played a lanista *in the film* Gladiator. *The men facing him are members of his stable of fighters.*

for the arena were special slave dealers called *lanistae*. A typical *lanista* traveled far and wide looking for slaves or prisoners he could buy cheaply and sell for the best possible profit. There were open slave auctions held in all the major cities and ports of the Mediterranean world. One of the biggest was located on the Greek island of Delos, where fresh supplies of slaves arrived each year from Thrace (the region north of the Aegean Sea), Asia Minor (now Turkey), and various parts of the Near East. Many *lanistae* frequented the Delian markets. Some also traded in the black market, run mainly by pirates who kidnapped

people from coastal villages and sold them as slaves.

At first, before state-run gladiator schools were established, the *lanistae* trained the gladiators themselves. It was not unusual for a *lanista* and/or his hired trainers to be former gladiators who knew the ropes of the profession. The *lanista*'s stable of fighters was called a *familia gladiatorum,* or "family of gladiators," members of which he could rent out or sell as he saw fit. Some customers in this market were prominent Romans who bought gladiators to fight at funerals; others were public officials, like Julius Caesar when he was aedile, who wanted to stage large public games featuring arena fighters.

By the end of the first century B.C., however, the Roman government had severely decreased the size of the lucrative role the *lanistae* played in the procurement of fighters for the arena. Following Caesar's large-scale presentation of gladiators in 65 B.C., the public games rapidly grew larger in scope and created a huge new demand for new gladiatorial recruits. Roman officials decided it was time to eliminate the middlemen, namely the *lanistae,* and exercise a monopoly on finding, maintaining, and training arena fighters.

The Roman government got its gladiatorial recruits from some of the same places the *lanistae* did. Roman officials bought slaves at markets in Delos and other ports, for instance. Some war captives were also forced into the arena. When the Roman army won a battle against a foreign people, government agents inspected the captives, selected the healthiest and strongest, and shipped them off to gladiator schools.

Another common way the government acquired new gladiatorial recruits was through the legal system. Both free persons and slaves convicted of serious crimes (such as arson or murder) sometimes received a penalty known as *damnatio ad ludum,* meaning "condemned to the gladiator barracks." Some of the condemned men may have hoped for this sentence. After all,

the alternative was immediate execution or hard labor in the mines, which practically guaranteed a slow and agonizing death.

The government had still other avenues for obtaining recruits for the arena. One was the old way—buying them from *lanistae,* a few of which still scratched out livings as best as they could. A *lanista* was now required to supply the person who administered a *munus*—the *editor*—with a certain number of recruits at a reasonable price. (Some Roman officials disliked dealing with *lanistae,* who were widely viewed as disreputable pimps, and turned to them only when absolutely necessary.) To make themselves some extra money, private slave owners also hired out or sold slaves to the *editores.* Such a slave had no choice but to obey his or her master and train to fight in the arena. This changed in the early second century A.D., however, when the emperor Hadrian altered the law. He made it so that a master was required either to get a slave's consent to become a gladiator or to present evidence that the slave had committed a serious crime.

FEMALE FIGHTERS

Whether they were free volunteers or unfree persons forced to train and fight, the vast majority of gladiators and other arena combatants were men. However, a few were women, particularly during the early Roman Empire (which began about 30 B.C.), a period in which certain emperors enjoyed seeing women fight in the *munera.* One was Domitian (who reigned from 81 to 96). Suetonius mentions games given by Domitian "by torchlight," that is, at night, "in which women as well as men took part."[8] An increasingly twisted individual as his reign progressed, Domitian also liked to see female gladiators fight male dwarfs.

In addition to a number of references in ancient written sources, a small but significant amount of archaeological evidence has been found for the woman gladiator, or gladiatrix. The most striking example is a relief sculpture carved on a stone slab found in the ruins of Halicarnassus, an ancient city in western Asia Minor. It shows two fe-

☙ THE SCANDAL OF FEMALE GLADIATORS ❧

Most Romans frowned on the idea of a woman, even of slave or other lower-class status, appearing in the arena. Therefore, when an upper-class lady assumed the mantle of gladiatrix, she was viewed with particular loathing. In his *Annals,* the first-century B.C. Roman historian Tacitus records that in the ninth year of Nero's reign (A.D. 63) Rome "witnessed gladiatorial dis-

plays on a no less magnificent scale than before, but exceeding all precedent in the number of distinguished women and senators disgracing themselves in the arena." Most evidence suggests that the tyrannical Nero forced most or all of these well-to-do persons to fight. So these women were probably not professional gladiators.

Archaeologists think the bones in the dishes are those of a female gladiator.

male gladiators standing and facing each other with their helmets removed. The women are armed with swords and rectangular shields just like those used by several types of male gladiators. The inscription accompanying the carving says, in effect, that the match between these two women ended in a draw, so both walked out of the arena alive. In the words of Graham Ashford, an expert on gladiatorial combats, "Of all the scant information left us about female gladiators, this is one of the most compelling as it shows they fought against other female fighters and were taken seriously enough to have a large stone carved in their honor."[9] The Halicarnassus carving also reveals the stage names of the two combatants. One was Achillia, a feminine form of Achilles, the warrior-hero of the *Iliad,* one of the two great epic poems of the Greek bard Homer; her opponent was Amazonia, named after the Amazons, the famous race of warrior women in Greco-Roman mythology.

The comparison of these female fighters to the legendary Amazons turns out to be revealing in more ways than one. Greek and Roman men almost unanimously agreed that the Amazons were unnatural, barbaric women because they controlled their own destiny rather than submitting to the control of men. Such independent women were viewed as potential threats to traditional male-dominated society in which females knew their place. And it was con-

The Halicarnassus carving, with the names of the female fighters inscribed below their feet.

sidered a sharp and demeaning insult to call a woman an Amazon. It is no wonder, then, that the gladiatrix was looked on as even more of a social outcast than the male gladiator. "We've all seen *them,*" Juvenal writes in a scathing attack on women gladiators,

stabbing the stump with a foil [sword], shield well advanced, going through the proper motions . . . unless they have higher ambitions, and the goal of all their practice is the real arena. But then, what modesty can be looked for in some helmeted vixen, a renegade from her sex, who thrives on masculine violence—yet would not prefer to *be* a man, since the pleasure is so much less? What a fine sight for some husband—*it might be you*—his wife's

GLADIATOR FIGHTS AS A SYMBOL OF ROMAN POWER

As they gained popularity, the Roman munera *became a symbol of Rome's power and civilizing influence, as explained here by scholar Alan Baker in his informative book on gladiators.*

The staging of gladiatorial contests spread with the Empire itself, and evidence of them has been found throughout the imperial territories. The popularity of the games in Rome meant that their presence further afield was seen as an important method of Romanizing conquered lands. Since Roman soldiers enjoyed watching gladiatorial contests, they would be staged for them in whatever new region they were occupying. To the people of ancient Rome, the arena of gladiatorial combat was a reflection of the awesome strength, power, and indeed civilization of their mighty Empire, whose territorial achievements had been secured through military violence.

equipment put up at auction, sword-belt, armlet, plumes [helmet decorations], and one odd shin-guard! Or, if the other style of fighting takes her fancy, imagine your delight when the dear girl sells off her greaves [lower leg protectors]! . . . Note how she snorts at each practice thrust, bowed down by the weight of her helmet . . . then wait for the laugh, when she lays down her weapons and squats over the potty![10]

Female gladiators were eventually banned from the Roman arena by the emperor Septimius Severus (reigned 193–211). Perhaps it was because he was an old-fashioned military man who felt that women should not at-tempt to fill men's roles. Or he may have been disturbed that increasing numbers of women had been joining the gladiatorial ranks in recent years.

HIS REPUTATION WENT WITH HIM

Although male gladiators survived their female counterparts in the arena for several centuries, their own low social status and that of their profession in general never improved. Indeed there was no way to become a gladiator without acquiring a bad reputation. The words of a second-century B.C. Latin writer, Calpurnius Flaccus, rang true for the entire five centuries or so in which gladiators played a major role in Roman public entertainment. "There is no meaner condition among the people," he said, "than that of the gladiator." [11]

Indeed, even after a gladiator left the profession his low reputation went with him. Of course, one way he might leave was to be killed in the arena. If he was more fortunate, he might survive for several years after a number of wins and draws, in which case his owner or the state might grant him his freedom for a job well done. Or he might save up enough prize money to buy his freedom. Either way, the gladiator could not escape who he was and the kind of work he had performed. Writers routinely slandered or poked fun at him and his colleagues, comparing them to criminals, prostitutes, actors, and other disreputable persons.

A gladiator's low social status even accompanied him in death. In a society in which proper burial was viewed as crucial to a person's dignity, gladiators' bodies were not allowed in public burial grounds. Some arena fighters did receive funerals, but only when family members, friends, or loyal fans claimed the bodies and buried them privately, often in unmarked graves. Unarguably, few professions in human history have affected so many aspects of a worker's life, death, and legacy as much as that of the gladiator.

CHAPTER 2

TRAINING FOR A DANGEROUS JOB

Ultimately, the work of the gladiator was to fight another person to the death in front of a crowd of spectators. This made the job extremely dangerous, and the only way to prepare for it was through rigorous training. By the early years of the Empire, the Roman government had acquired a monopoly on gladiatorial shows. Likewise, the state erected and managed the only authorized schools for training gladiators and other arena fighters—the *ludi* (short for *ludi gladiatoria,* meaning "barracks for gladiators"). In these facilities, the arena fighters endured months or years of harsh training and discipline and highly regimented lives.

THE IMPERIAL TRAINING SCHOOLS

The city of Rome had four imperial *ludi.* Because they were located in the capital, they were the most prestigious in the Empire, just as the public games presented in Rome were the most renowned and glamorous. The four schools were the *Ludus Gallicus, Ludus Dacicus, Ludus Magnus,* and *Ludus Matutinus.* The first three trained regular gladiators, and the fourth specialized in preparing the fighters whose job was to confront wild beasts in the arena.

Probably the largest and most important of the four *ludi* in the capital was the *Ludus Magnus,* begun by Domitian and completed by Hadrian a few decades later. The facility was located near the Colosseum, the largest amphitheater in the Empire. (Amphitheaters were huge oval-shaped structures built to house the *munera* and wild animal fights. The first stone version was erected in Pompeii in the early first century B.C., and the Colosseum was completed in the early 80s A.D.) The *Ludus Magnus* and the Colosseum were connected by an underground tunnel, which allowed the fighters to move from one facility to the other without being seen by the public.

The *Ludus Magnus* itself had its own fighting arena, which was considerably smaller than that of the Colosseum. The school's arena was surrounded by seats for about three thousand spectators (as compared to fifty thousand for the Colosseum). It was not unusual for interested citizens to spend a few of their leisure hours in these seats watching the gladiators train (in the same way that modern baseball fans watch the players during spring training). On the outside rim of the school's arena rose a structure three stories high, each level featuring a series of small brick cubicles. These were the cells where the trainees slept.

There were also imperial *ludi* in other parts of Italy as well as in most or perhaps all of Rome's provinces. Ravenna, in northern Italy, had one, as did Capua, on the southwestern coast of the peninsula. The large city of Alexandria, in the province of Egypt, also had a gladiator school. The best preserved of these schools, thanks to the eruption of

The rectangular training ground of the gladiatorial barracks at Pompeii, preserved by a thick blanket of volcanic ash.

Mount Vesuvius in A.D. 79, is the one in Pompeii. According to Michael Grant:

> Nearly a hundred rooms were grouped round a rectangular space of some 53 by 42 meters [174 by 138 feet]. Some of them were on an upper floor, reached by a staircase leading up to a wooden gallery, of which part has now been reconstructed. The cells on the two floors are between three and four meters [ten and thirteen feet] square, without windows; these were the grim, dark, and dank quarters in which gladiators had to live. On their premises at Pompeii were found sixty-three skeletons of people who lost their lives in the eruption of Vesuvius. [12]

SWEARING TO DIE LIKE A SOLDIER

Each of the gladiator schools in Italy was run by an official known as a *procurator*. In the provinces, by contrast, a *procurator* oversaw all the schools in his province. This official had complete authority over all aspects of the trainees' lives while they were in his charge; he decided when and how long they drilled and practiced, what and when they ate, how long they slept, and the severity of their punishment when they broke the rules.

The *procurator* laid down these rules to the new recruits when they first en-

tered his school. The details of the induction ceremony are unknown. It appears certain, though, that at one point the recruits swore the gladiatorial oath, which probably went something like this: "I swear to be burned, to be bound, to be beaten, [and] to die by the sword." The reason that this remains an approximation of the oath is that the exact words have not survived, or at least have not yet been discovered.

Fortunately, some paraphrases of the oath appear in the works of a few ancient writers. One is the thirty-seventh epistle (letter) in the *Moral Letters* of the first-century Roman philosopher Seneca the Younger. Seneca compared the oath of a gladiator, spoken unwillingly, to that of a soldier, whom the writer naturally viewed as more virtuous.

> You [a soldier] have ... enlisted under oath.... I will not have you deceived. The words of this most honorable compact are the same as the words of that most disgraceful one, to wit: "through burning, imprisonment, or death by the sword." From the men who hire out their strength for the arena ... security is taken that they will endure such trials even though they be unwilling; from you, that you will endure them willingly.... The gladiator may lower his weapon and test the pity of the people; but you will neither lower your weapon nor beg for

Gladiators raise their weapons to salute the emperor Nero, played by Charles Laughton in Cecil B. DeMille's film The Sign of the Cross.

life. You must die erect and unyielding. [13]

Seneca's comparison of the oaths of gladiators and soldiers shows how the Roman double standard about gladia-tors affected the lives of the recruits from the moment they entered a training school. The trainees had to promise to die like Roman soldiers. Yet the recruits were denied the status, civil rights, and especially the freedom of

PETRONIUS MENTIONS THE GLADIATOR'S OATH

In addition to Seneca's mention of the gladiator's oath, the Roman writer Petronius also included a paraphrase of the oath in the Satyricon, *a novel in which three unscrupulous young men get involved in adventures while traveling through southern Italy. At one point, the youths pretend they are the slaves of another man, Eumolpus, and they mimic gladiators swearing loyalty to their owner:*

To safeguard the imposture [charade] in which we were all involved, we swore an oath dictated by Eumolpus, that we would be burned, flogged, beaten, killed with cold steel or whatever else Eumolpus ordered. Like real gladiators we very solemnly handed ourselves over, body and soul, to our master. After swearing the oath, we saluted our master in our role as slaves.

choice enjoyed by soldiers. Indeed, in swearing the oath on his first day in a *ludus,* a gladiator had no choice but to transfer complete control of his own destiny to the *procurator,* the games *editor,* and ultimately the spectators, all of whom society deemed his "betters."

HARSH CONDITIONS AND THE THREAT OF ESCAPE

After the induction ceremony, the recruits settled down to the repetitious, monotonous, and physically and mentally demanding routine of training for the arena. Living conditions were harsh by modern standards. The typical cubicle in which a trainee slept was twelve feet square at most and probably provided only a makeshift mattress consisting of a pile of straw covered by a woolen blanket. There were no openings between the cells, so the inmates could not see one another; nor were they allowed to converse (although some likely found ways to subvert this rule).

The trainees were allowed to leave their cells at mealtimes. Under guard, they filed through dimly lit corridors to the school's kitchen and dining area, which was more or less centrally located. In the Pompeiian *ludus,* for example, the kitchen ran along the entire length of one side of the central practice area. The kitchen had a large stone hearth on which cooks heated food in big metal pots. Not only was the food nutritious, there was plenty of it, as the aim of the institution was to turn out strong, hearty fighters.

It is unknown what and how much rule breakers ate during their tenure in the facility's on-site prison. It is possible that these unfortunate individuals subsisted on bread and water while enduring the extremely uncomfortable physical conditions. The prison in the gladiator school at Pompeii had a ceiling so low that the inmates could not stand. They must have spent long hours and days lying down, their legs held fast in painful iron shackles.

Such harsh living conditions and punishments were deemed necessary to keep hundreds of strong, potentially dangerous men in line. The *procurator* lived constantly with the worry that one or more of the inmates might escape, which the state would see as a black mark against both the facility and its director. For this reason, great care was taken to make sure the inmates had no access to weapons when they were away from the training area.

This included knives, cleavers, and other kitchen tools that might be used

Gladiator trainees toughen themselves by running with heavy timbers in a scene deleted from the final cut of Stanley Kubrick's 1960 film, Spartacus.

as weapons. *Procuratores* always took care to lecture their guards about how such kitchen implements had been instrumental in the famous escape from a privately run *ludus* near Capua in 73 B.C. This event, the memory of which haunted the Roman government ever after, was the initial spark of the famous gladiator-slave rebellion of a Thracian trainee named Spartacus. According to the first-century A.D. Greek writer Plutarch:

> The rising of the gladiators and their devastation of Italy, which is generally known as the War of Spartacus, began as follows. A man called Lentulus Batiatus had an establishment for gladiators at Capua. . . . Because of the cruelty of their owner [they] were kept in close confinement. . . . Two hundred of them planned to escape, but their plan was betrayed and only seventy-eight . . . managed to act in time and get away, armed

with choppers and spits which they seized from [the] cookhouse. [14]

After escaping, Spartacus and his men terrorized the surrounding countryside and eventually freed many slaves in Italy. The gladiators trained a large number of ordinary slaves to fight effectively and thereby created a formidable military force that managed to defeat several small Roman armies. Finally, however, the rebels faced the full force of the Roman military and were annihilated.

ON THE TRAINING FIELD

After the Spartacus fiasco, gladiator schools, including the imperial *ludi,* installed rigid safeguards (which worked, since thereafter no other large-scale escapes were ever successful). The most opportune time for such escapes was during the actual training sessions, when the recruits were armed. To make sure there was no trouble, the entire perimeter of the training area was lined

---

✑ PLUTARCH DESCRIBES SPARTACUS ✑

In his Life of Crassus *(quoted in Rex Warner's* Fall of the Roman Republic *), Plutarch describes Spartacus's personal attributes, saying that he*

not only had a great spirit and great physical strength, but was, much more

than one would expect from his condition [i.e., that he was a lowly slave and gladiator], most intelligent and cultured, being more like a Greek than a Thracian . . . . His wife . . . came from the same tribe and . . . shared in his escape and was then living with him.

Modern reenactors strike at the wooden pole known as the palus *to demonstrate part of the training regimen of Roman gladiators.*

with soldiers in full armor. At the slightest sign of trouble, they captured or killed the perpetrators, and more soldiers stationed on the outside of the facility blocked all possible exits.

The recruits had no choice, therefore, but to undergo the comprehensive and rigorous course of training without complaint. Each of their instructors, called *doctores,* specialized in a specific kind of weapon or fighting style. As had been the case in the training camps of the *lanistae,* these instructors were former gladiators with considerable expertise. The *doctores* barked orders and insults at the trainees, correcting mistakes made in footwork, offensive moves, defensive parries, and so forth.

At first, the trainees attacked a stationary six-foot-tall wooden pole called the *palus.* They used a wooden sword, the *rudis,* to strike at the pole, which could be rigged with heavy weights that

swung around and hit them if they did not dodge quickly enough. These drills helped develop better reflexes and hand-to-eye coordination, which a gladiator had to possess to become successful in his dangerous profession. The word *palus* also denoted one of several teams or squads of trainees. The most skilled and respected team in a school was the *primus palus,* the second best was the *secundus palus,* and so forth. Such teams regularly squared off against one another to encourage a spirit of competitive rivalry.

The members of the teams did not clash all at once in groups, however. Instead, one person from one team met one from another team in single combat, the main fighting style they would later use as full-fledged gladiators in the arena. Closely watched and coached by the *doctores,* the trainees, armed with training swords and shields, drilled in

In a fight between modern gladiator reenactors, the man at right adopts the classic stance to guard against his attacker.

the basic moves of attack and defense. Perhaps the most basic of all was the classic stance, often adopted by fighters wielding the standard thrusting sword and rectangular shield used by Roman soldiers. (Fighters with other kinds of weapons and shields used modified versions of the classic stance.)

To make the classic stance effective, the fighter needed to take full advantage of the cover provided by the shield. According to Graham Ashford, who has conducted many authentic reconstructions of ancient gladiatorial fights, the gladiator held the shield with his left arm in such a way that the shield lay flat against and protected the torso and upper left thigh. The fighter planted the right leg farther back and distributed his or her weight evenly across both feet. "The right arm," says Ashford, stayed "behind the shield with either the front end of the sword facing out to the ene-

my or hidden behind the shield to hide the sword's full length and position." [15]

From this highly protective stance, a fighter could keep a close eye on his opponent while formulating his own plan of attack. Whatever his offensive strategy might be, until it was launched it was vital to remain well protected in the classic stance. To that end, Ashford points out,

> the position of the body to the shield [was] pivotal. By holding the [shield] slightly above shoulder height the gladiator . . . [was] able to see everything that his enemy [was] doing while hiding much of his own movements. Also, he [could] defend his shoulders without any movement at all. [16]

In addition to the classic stance and perhaps other defensive postures, the

✍ SPARTACUS ON FILM ✍

One of the most accurately costumed and staged versions of a gladiator fight in modern movies occurs in the 1960 film *Spartacus.* The opening scenes of the film depict the trials of the title character (played by Kirk Douglas) after arriving in chains at the gladiator school of Lentulus Batiatus, near Capua. Forced to fight a fellow trainee in the facility's small arena, Spartacus is outfitted as a Thracian. His chest is bare and he wields a round shield *(parma)* and curved sword *(sica),* although his helmet is missing, probably to allow the film audience a better view of the actor's facial expressions. Spartacus's opponent is a *retiarius,* armed with a net and trident. The scene effectively re-creates the spectacle, excitement, and brutality of the Roman arena.

Spartacus (Kirk Douglas), at right, and a fellow trainee (Woody Strode) prepare to grapple in the arena scene from Spartacus.

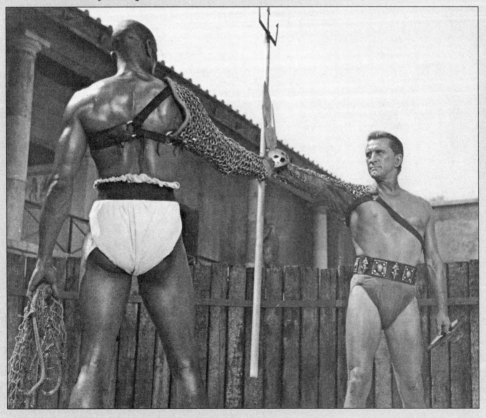

gladiators learned the various forms of attack they would use later in the arena. With their wooden swords, they drilled relentlessly in these moves because, as the *doctores* frequently reminded them, their lives would eventually depend on their correct execution.

THE BEST HEALTH CARE AVAILABLE

Even though the trainees used wooden swords most of the time, the successful strikes they made during these practice combats were delivered with full force. So minor injuries were prob-ably common. (Some evidence suggests that near the end of the training period the fighters were given metal swords, although with blunted points; if so, some injuries may have been more serious.)

Fortunately, such injuries were immediately and expertly treated, for the *ludi* had some of the best physicians available on their staffs. For example, Galen, the foremost medical practitioner in Rome's history, began his career as a doctor to gladiators in the Greek city of Pergamum. (Tending to their sometimes serious wounds taught

In this scene from the 1962 film Barabbas, *the title character (played by Anthony Quinn) performs agility drills in a gladiator school.*

A modern drawing shows the renowned doctor Galen treating a gladiator's wounds.

him a great deal about internal human anatomy. This was important because at the time dissecting human bodies was forbidden.)

Good medical treatment was part of an overall program of first-rate health care for experienced gladiators and trainees alike. In addition to supplying good doctors, the schools themselves were carefully located in warm, dry climates that discouraged illness and promoted rapid recovery; and specialists kept a watchful eye on the inmates' diets. Such meticulous care was not motivated by humanitarian concerns but rather by financial ones. From the government's point of view, the fighters constituted a major capital investment in the form of valuable property that must be well maintained. Ironically, therefore, the Roman profession that held human life the cheapest also provided the best health care then available, and for free.

CHAPTER 3

THE ELABORATE PRESHOW CEREMONIES

In the dual role of fighter and showman, a gladiator provided a crowd of spectators with entertainment. The show consisted of more than the actual fighting, however. As part of the job, gladiators were also obligated to entertain the public *before* the combats in a series of elaborate preshow ceremonies. This included a formal public introduction of the fighters two days prior to their scheduled matches, a banquet the night before, a colorful parade around the arena, and other events.

To the crowds who watched, these events constituted an accepted and eagerly anticipated part of the spectacle of the Roman games. The gladiators themselves likely viewed this part of the job with mixed feelings, however. Some evidence suggests that they enjoyed being the center of attention, however briefly, because it made them feel special; for that fleeting moment in their lives, they enjoyed almost the same kind of adulation given to Roman soldiers returning home after a victory.

In contrast, other gladiators may have viewed the preshow ceremony as degrading and exploitive. Despite the pomp and ceremony, they probably could not forget that they were captives forced against their will to take part in public displays that might well culminate in their own deaths. Yet they remained silent because they knew that resistance or protest of any kind would be futile, as well as a stain on their honor. No matter how distasteful, showmanship was part of a gladiator's work. And if they were fated to die shortly, they may have wanted to be remembered as professionals who did their jobs without complaint.

ADVERTISING UPCOMING COMBATS

The first aspect of the preshow activities —advertising the upcoming *munus*—did not directly involve the gladiators; yet they were indirectly affected by it because the ads brought in many of the spectators who would help decide whether the fighters would live or die. No radio, television, or other mass media yet existed; so the ads, called *edicta,* were painted on the walls of buildings or on the sides of roadside tombs, especially in areas with heavy foot and cart traffic. Usually, the ads were executed by professional scribes or sign painters,

Gladiators march in a parade held before the arena bouts. Part of the fighters' job was to entertain the public with preshow events.

who employed bright colors to make their messages stand out from the ordinary graffiti that cluttered the walls. One of these painters, Aemilius Celer, left his calling card in the following ad on a wall in Pompeii:

> Twenty pairs of gladiators sponsored by Decimus Lucretius Satirus Valens, lifetime priest of Nero Caesar [i.e., a priest of the local cult that worshipped the emperor as a semidivine being], and ten pairs of gladiators sponsored by Decimus Lucretius Valens, his son, will fight in Pompeii on April 8, 9, 10, 11, and 12. There will also be a suitable wild animal hunt. The awnings will be used. Aemilius Celer wrote this, all alone, in the moonlight. [17]

This ad was fairly typical in that it provided the public with certain basic facts about the impending *munus.* It identified the sponsor or sponsors, for instance, in this case a noted local businessman and his son. It also told how many gladiators would be fighting, where and when the combats would take place, and what other events would be featured on the program (in this case, an animal show). In addition, it was customary to mention any amenities offered for the spectators' comfort. The awning touted in the ad was a canvas tarp that could be rigged to cover the open top of the amphitheater to keep the audience from baking in the hot Mediterranean sun. The awning also figured prominently in another, shorter ad found at Pompeii: "The gladiatorial troop hired by Aulus Suettius Certus will fight in Pompeii on May 31. There will also be a wild animal hunt. The awnings will be used." [18]

When the sponsor of the games could afford it, he hired artists to create more elaborate *edicta,* sometimes including likenesses of the gladiators who would be fighting in the upcoming *munus.* According to the noted first-century A.D. Roman scholar and encyclopedist Pliny the Elder:

⚜ WINNERS AND LOSERS ⚜

In addition to ads (edicta) promoting upcoming gladiatorial bouts, sometimes the results of past matches were painted on city walls. The following examples (translated by Jo-Ann Shelton in her As the Romans Did*), found at Pompeii, describe the outcomes of two bouts.*

Oceanus, a freedman, winner of 13 matches, won. Aracintus, a freedman, winner of 9 matches, lost. Severus, a freedman, winner of 13 matches, lost. Albanus, a freedman of Scaurus, winner of 19 matches, won.

The cena libera, *a banquet gladiators attended the night before their matches, is reenacted in the 1954 film* Demetrius and the Gladiators.

When a freedman of [the emperor] Nero was putting on a gladiatorial show at Antium, paintings containing life-like portraits of all the gladiators and their assistants decorated the public porticoes [roofed walkways]. Portraits of gladiators have commanded the greatest interest in art for many generations. It was, however, Gaius Terentius Lucanus who began commissioning pictures of gladiatorial shows and having them publicly exhibited. [19]

MEETING THE PUBLIC

The next part of the preshow ceremony featured the gladiators in the flesh. Usually about two days before the scheduled *munus,* the *editor* drummed up more interest for the event by introducing the fighters to the public. This commonly took place in a crowded public place, most often a city forum or marketplace. The exact manner of these introductions is unknown. But it is probable that the gladiators stood on a raised platform and stepped forward one by one as the *editor* called out their names and cited their record of victories, if any. The more famous contestants likely received huge rounds of applause and cheers.

Selected members of the public got another chance to view the gladiators the next night, on the eve of the *munus.* The sponsor of the event threw a lavish banquet for the fighters, the *cena libera* (which translates as "free supper"). This vivid description of the feast by the late classical scholar Jerome Carcopino is based on ancient evidence:

The public was admitted to the *cena libera,* and the curious circulated round the tables with unwholesome joy. Some of the [more fatalistic gladiators] . . . abandoned themselves to the pleasures of the moment and ate gluttonously. Others, anxious to increase their chances by taking thought for their health, resisted the temptations of the generous fare and ate with moderation. The most wretched, haunted by [worries about] approaching death, their throats and bellies already paralyzed by fear, gave way to lamentation . . . and made their last will and testament. [20]

During or perhaps after the banquet, the *editor's* agents made detailed programs available to the public. Such a program, called a *libellus munerarius,* listed all the gladiators who would appear in the arena the next day, along with the number of wins and draws, if any, they had accumulated in their careers. A few of the names listed were the fighters' real names. But most were colorful stage names like those adopted by modern professional boxers and wrestlers. Typical men's stage names were Tigris ("Tiger"), Pugnax ("the Feisty One"), and Hermes (the Greek version of Mercury, the Roman god thought to lead the souls of the dead into the Underworld).

THE PARADE AND SALUTE

The next day, those citizens who had been waiting eagerly to see the *munus* be-

gan filing into the amphitheater. If animal fights were also to be presented, which was the case more often than not, they usually took place before the gladiatorial combats. So the stands were filled with spectators well before the gladiators arrived. Full houses for the *munera* were virtually guaranteed, as these games were widely popular and not presented on a regular basis. (During the Empire, most amphitheaters featured them fewer than ten times a year, mainly because they were so expensive to stage.) As the fans waited for the gladiators to arrive, they lounged on cushions, which made sitting on the stone seats bearable; they also snacked on food sold by roving vendors or purchased from nearby bakeries and cookshops.

Finally, an orchestra composed of trumpets, flutes, drums, and a large hydraulic organ delivered a rousing fanfare, followed by marching music. This was the signal for the opening ceremonies of the *munus* to begin. As the music continued, marchers in a colorful parade called the *pompa* began to enter the amphitheater's main gate. First came two *lictores,* attendants who always accompanied high government officials in public; in this case, they attended the *editor* of the games. Over their shoulders, the *lictores* carried the *fasces,* an ax enclosed by a bundle of sticks, which symbolized the power of Rome. Other attendants followed, and then came the *editor* himself, attired in a magnificent gold-fringed toga. Next came men bear-

The Roman emperor Commodus, who fancied himself an arena hero, participates in a pompa *preceding one of the many gladiatorial events he sponsored.*

ing the gladiators' weapons as well as acrobats, jugglers, and other circuslike performers, who skipped and gyrated to the music.

At last came the gladiators, decked out in their impressive armor. A loud, sustained cheer rang out from the bleachers, for this was what the crowd had been waiting for most anxiously. The wave of adulation must have lifted the fighters' spirits, at least momentarily. Modern scholars believe that gladiators tried not to register any emotion during their fights. From the moment they stepped onto the arena's sands, they were, as they had been trained to be, all business, and they marched along to the music with stoic expressions.

The climax of the *pompa* likely came when the ranks of gladiators reached the part of the arena directly below the special box seats reserved for high officials. (In the Colosseum in Rome, the emperor sat here; in other cities it might be a governor, an important local person, or a visiting dignitary.) At this point, the music and procession stopped and the fighters, in unison, gave a formal salute to the official in the box. *"Morituri te salutant!"* they shouted, essentially meaning "Those who are about to die salute you!"

The words of this now-famous salute were recorded for posterity by the historian Suetonius in his biography of the fourth emperor, Claudius (reigned 41–54). According to Suetonius, Claudius

CLAUDIUS'S ATTEMPT AT HUMOR BACKFIRES

This is the full passage from Suetonius's biography of Claudius, found in The Twelve Caesars, *in which Claudius had a disagreement with the fighters in one of his games:*

Among the many gladiatorial games presented by him [Claudius] in various places was . . . a sham seafight on [the Fucine Lake]; but when the gladiators shouted: "Hail Caesar, we salute you, we who are about to die!" he answered: "Or not, as the case may be."

They unanimously took him up on this and refused to fight, insisting that his words amounted to a pardon. Claudius grew so angry that he was on the point of sending troops to massacre them all, or burning them in their ships; however, he changed his mind, jumped from his throne and, hobbling ridiculously down to the lakeside, threatened and coaxed the gladiators into battle. Twelve Rhodian triremes [warships] then engaged twelve Sicilian ones.

was presenting a mock sea battle on a lake near Rome. And just prior to the commencement of combat, the fighters recited the salute, just as gladiators did before their arena bouts. However, Claudius made the mistake of answering the salute with an attempt at the simpleminded humor for which he was well known. He shouted back: "Or not, as the case may be!" But he soon regretted it, for as Suetonius writes, the combatants

unanimously took him up on this and refused to fight, insisting that his words amounted to a pardon. Claudius grew so angry that he was on the point of sending troops to massacre them all, or burning them

in their ships; however, he changed his mind, jumped from his throne and, hobbling ridiculously down to the lakeside, threatened and coaxed the gladiators into battle. [21]

It is doubtful that such a large-scale display of insubordination ever occurred in the *munera* since it stands to reason that some Roman writer would have recorded it. Perhaps Claudius's successors learned from his mistake and always greeted the gladiators' salute with a simple nod or wave of the hand.

THE LOTTERY AND TEST OF ARMS

After the *pompa* was over, it was time for some preliminary, bloodless bouts to whet the audience's appetite and perhaps to allow the gladiators to warm up for the real matches to come. The first of these preshow matches were performed by mock fighters known as *paegniarii*. Very little is known about them or their bouts. But scattered artistic depictions and remarks in ancient literary works suggest that they were comical in theme and style. A Roman mosaic found in Germany, for example, shows a *paegniarius* using a whip to attack his opponent, who fends him off with a stick. And Suetonius mentions that during some *munera* the cruel emperor Caligula liked to "stage comic duels between respectable householders who happened to be physically disabled in some way or other." [22] It is possible that some of the circuslike performers who entered the arena during the *pompa* also took part in these comic matches.

Next came preliminary bouts of a different sort—the *prolusiones,* performed by fighters called *lusorii.* These mock battles displayed the actual moves of gladiators, except that the participants wielded wooden swords like those used by the trainees in the *ludi.* Because of a scarcity of evidence, it remains unclear whether the *lusorii* were the gladiators themselves engaging in warm-ups or other performers standing in for them.

The gladiators definitely had no stand-ins for the next event in the preshow ceremony. It consisted of a lottery to decide who would fight whom and in what order. With only occasional exceptions, the combatants were paired in one-on-one combats. The games *editor* took charge of the lottery, in which the gladiators drew premarked objects, perhaps colored stones, from a receptacle. There may have been separate drawings based on the fighters' differing levels of experience. It is likely, for instance, that experienced veterans drew only against other veterans, and novices drew only against fellow novices. "There would have been no point in opposing a veteran of the arena," scholar Roland Auguet points out, "and some novice who had not yet had even a single victory. Furthermore, the gladiator himself would have judged it dishonorable to be paired with an adversary not of his stature." [23]

Apparently, there were rare but notable exceptions to this rule. According to scholar Marcus Junkelmann:

> A talented and ambitious beginner could be very dangerous to a veteran, as various inscriptions make clear. For instance, a graffito from Pompeii records a fight between . . . Marcus Attilius . . . making his first appearance [in the arena], and . . . Hilarus . . . a veteran who had already won fourteen victories. [24]

Not only did Attilius, the novice, win the match, he went on in his next fight to defeat a twelve-time winner named Lucius Raecius Felix.

❧ ROMAN ORCHESTRAS ❧

Roman orchestras played not only in the *munera* but also for theatrical plays, balletlike presentations, religious festivals, weddings, feasts, military victory parades, and other public events. The instruments consisted of various kinds of harps, guitarlike devices, bladders that were blown into like bagpipes, flutes, brass trumpets and tubas, drums, cymbals, tambourines, rattles, and pipe organs of various sizes. Sometimes choirs of singers accompanied the orchestras. Several Roman writers, notably the playwright Seneca the Younger and the orator Quintilian, mention the use of large musical ensembles in the introductory parades at the *munera*. And some evidence suggests that the musicians also played during the combats, providing background music similar to that used to heighten the drama in modern movies.

A nineteenth-century engraving shows Roman musicians accompanying a theatrical presentation.

Once the pairings and order of matches were decided, the *editor* ordered the gladiators to line up and receive their weapons. Once they were armed, he (or some distinguished guest or even the emperor himself if he was present) inspected these weapons. The process, known as the *probatio armorum,* meaning "proof" or "test" of arms, was intended to ensure that the weapons were sound and well sharpened. As Alan Baker points out, this was no trivial matter:

Far from being bored by this meticulous inspection, most members of the crowd watched it with great attentiveness, for it ensured that all the gladiators would be fighting with the very best weapons, and thus that each contest would be decided by the skill of the fighters rather than the quality of their tools. [25]

The test of arms was the last of the preshow events. The gladiators were now warmed up, armed, and ready to engage in their primary work— the grim struggle to kill or be killed.

CHAPTER 4

DIFFERENT WEAPONS AND FIGHTING STYLES

The gladiators who marched into the amphitheater in the *pompa* and drew lots to decide who would fight whom were a motley crew to say the least. Many different types of arena combatants existed, each of whom bore specific armor and weapons and fought in a distinct style. Because surviving evidence is scattered and scarce, the exact number of these separate types is unknown. Twenty or more may have existed. Or there may have been as few as six or seven, with some having minor variations that to the modern eye look like distinct types.

What is certain is that the main objective of each gladiator type was the same—to kill one's opponent and win the match; however, each went about it in a different way. The resulting variety made the *munera* more colorful and entertaining for the spectators. At the same time, it added levels of specialization, complexity, and difficulty to the gladi-

atorial profession itself. To be successful, a fighter had not only to master his own weapons but also to learn to defend against opponents attacking with markedly different weapons.

The considerable variety of arena fighters also reflected the use of the gladiatorial profession as a tool to express Roman nationalism and propaganda. Each kind of gladiator represented a warrior of a specific foreign people that the Roman army had once fought and defeated. In the combats in the Colosseum and in other Roman amphitheaters, these foreigners were symbolically reduced to miserable slaves forced to fight one another to the death before the "superior" Romans. Able to decide the life or death of the fighters with a turn of the thumb, everyday Romans were able to publicly express feelings of pride in their nation, its achievements, and its invincibility. Thus, part of a gladiator's work was to make the spectators feel better about themselves.

DESCENDANTS OF THE SAMNITE

This symbolic subjugation of foreign peoples in the arena can be seen clearly in the case of the first-known gladiator type, which may have been the only one for a century or more. This was the Samnite, whose armor and weapons were copied from Samnite warriors of the fourth century B.C. The Romans long viewed their final victory over the Samnites as a great accomplishment and test of their national will; and placing the enemy in the subordinate role of the gladiator helped remind Rome that it had passed that supreme test with distinction. The Samnite gladiator wielded a thrusting sword and rectangular shield that were adopted by Roman soldiers. He also wore a metal helmet and a greave (metal leg armor) on one leg. The helmet had a visor with several small perforations across the face, a wide brim above the visor, and a small crested dome at the top.

Eventually, by the early years of the Empire, the Samnite was phased out of the *munera*. At about the same time, several kinds of gladiators similar to the Samnite in appearance and fighting style were introduced; it seems likely that they were variations or spinoffs of the Samnite. Among these was the *secutor.* He wore a visored helmet that was more rounded and protected the face

better than that of a Samnite; the *secutor's* helmet also had two round eyeholes instead of smaller perforations. This distinction may have been enough to classify the *secutor* as a separate gladiator type. Perhaps the *secutor* was distinguished more by who he opposed in the arena. His name means "pursuer," and it is possible that his distinction lay

The Samnite gladiator as he appeared in full battle array.

in the fact that he traditionally fought a less-armored gladiator who fought with a net.

Another gladiator type who looked much like the Samnite and the *secutor* was the *myrmillo,* or "fish-man." He was named for the *mormylos,* a fish that appeared in an elaborate crest on the front of his Samnite-like helmet. Like the Samnite and the *secutor,* the *myrmillo* carried a rectangular shield, the *scutum.* In addition to his helmet and shield, the *myrmillo* wore a single greave (or perhaps sometimes two), and a single *manica,* an arm guard made of layers of leather or linen.

It is important to emphasize that the Samnite gladiator and his descendants did not wear cuirasses (chest protectors), as Roman soldiers did. Instead,

members of this class of arena fighter, along with most others, were naked above the waist and had only a loincloth and short cloth skirt to cover the groin area. There was usually a marked difference, therefore, between the high degree of protection of a fighter's limbs and the complete lack of protection of his torso. According to Alan Baker, "The purpose behind this arrangement was to prolong the fight as much as possible. Without adequate protection on his limbs, a fighter could be quickly incapacitated by a non-lethal blow, which was considered undesirable." [26]

OTHER MAJOR GLADIATOR TYPES

Like the gladiators in the Samnite class, another heavily armed arena fighter,

A Roman mosaic found in North Africa depicts various kinds of gladiators—a retiarius *(at far left), a Samnite, and several Samnite-like warriors.*

the *hoplomachus,* wore a visored Samnite-like helmet and fought bare chested. However, the array of weaponry wielded by the *hoplomachus* was somewhat different than that of the Samnite and the *secutor.* Although the *hoplomachus* wielded the standard short sword, the *gladius,* he also carried a spear or lance. In addition, his shield was not rectangular but round. These facts, combined with his name, suggest that the *hoplomachus* was meant to represent the Greek hoplite, a heavily armored infantry soldier who fought with a thrusting spear, backed up by a short sword and round shield, sometimes called the *hoplon.* It appears that in combat a *hoplomachus* was most often paired with a *myrmillo.*

Another gladiator who often fought *myrmillones* and who resembled the *hoplomachus* in a number of ways was the

Thracian (*thrax*). As his name suggests, the Thracian, another bare-chested fighter, was named after warriors from Thrace. He bore a curved short sword, the *sica,* and a small round or rectangular shield, the *parma* (or *parmula*). And his legs were protected by *fasciae,* strips of leather or cloth wound around the thighs, as well as by two bronze greaves. The Thracian's helmet resembled that of the Samnite and the *myrmillo* except that it featured an ornament shaped like a mythological creature, the griffin, companion to Nemesis, goddess of fate.

Still another distinctive gladiator was the *retiarius,* who also fought *myrmillones,* but was more often pitted against *secutores. Retiarius* means "net-man," a reference to the fact that he wielded a rope net (the *rete*) with which he tried to ensnare or at least trip his adversary. The net was equipped with weights, scholar Stephen Wisdom writes,

> like modern fishing weights and if lashed with sufficient power, the net could blind a man. Around the perimeter of the net was a rope, both ends of which were tied to the wrist of the *retiarius.* If thrown unnecessarily, he could jerk the net back into his grip.[27]

The *retiarius* carried no shield. Instead, he brandished a long trident or harpoon (the *fascina*), with three sharp barbs, and a dagger. If his opponent grabbed hold

A retiarius *(with net and trident) fights a* myrmillo *in an arena bout from the movie* Barabbas. *These two types were often pitted against each other.*

of his net and threw him off balance, he likely used the dagger to cut himself free and then attacked with his trident.

References in ancient literature suggest that the *retiarius* did not have the same status or command the same respect as most other gladiators. For example, his living quarters in the *ludus* were the smallest and most uncomfortable. Although the exact reasons for this discrimination are unclear, it is possible that it derived from the *retiarius's*

lack of armor. The Romans idolized their heavily armored soldiers, who were seen as "real men." So society may have associated armor with manliness. In contrast, a fighter who wore no armor was probably viewed as unmanly, perhaps even cowardly. The image of the *retiarius* as a coward may have been reinforced by his tactics in the arena. Out of necessity, because he had no shield or significant body armor, he tended to back away from an opponent more often than he attacked; and if he lost his net and trident, he had no choice but to run.

Still, it was not always the *retiarius* who ended up running away during combat. Most Romans were familiar with a popular tale connected to the traditional rivalry between *myrmillones* and *retiarii*. In this story, a *myrmillo* retreated from a net-man, who yelled, "It is not you I am trying to catch, it's your fish [a reference to the fish crest on the man's helmet]; why do you run away?" [28]

SOME UNUSUAL GLADIATOR TYPES

In addition to these major kinds of gladiators and the common ways they were paired (for example, *myrmillo* versus *hoplomachus* and *retiarius* versus *secutor*), the *munera* featured a number of

---

ॐ RIDICULE FOR A *RETIARIUS* ॐ

It is not completely clear why the retiarius *occupied a low level in the gladiatorial pecking order. There is no doubt, though, that some ancient writers often ridiculed this gladiator type. In one of his satires (quoted here from Peter Green's translation), Juvenal had harsh words for a descendant of one of Rome's noblest families who had decided to volunteer as a* retiarius:

The games! Go there for the ultimate scandal. Look at Gracchus who fights, but not with the arms of a swordsmen, not with a dagger or shield (he hates and despises such weapons), nor does a helmet hide his face. What he holds is a trident. What he hurls is a net, and he misses, of course, and we see him look up at the seats, then run for his life, all around the arena, easy for all to know and identify. Look at his tunic, golden cord and fringe, and that queer conspicuous arm guard!

Richard Egan plays the role of a retiarius *in* Demetrius and the Gladiators.

❧ THE MIGHTY COLOSSEUM ❧

The most famous of all the facilities that housed the Roman *munera* was the Colosseum. Its original name was the Amphitheatrum Flavium, or "Amphitheater of the Flavians," a reference to the Flavian family of rulers—Vespasian, Titus, and Domitian—who erected it. (The name Colosseum did not come into general use until early medieval times.) Vespasian began construction; most of the main features were completed by the summer of 80, during Titus's reign; and the finishing touches were added after his untimely death in September of the following year, when Domitian became emperor. In its original majesty, the building's oval bowl measured 620 by 513 feet in breadth and over 156 feet in height. The oval arena floor was 287 feet long by 180 feet wide. Because the structure's seating sections no longer exist, the exact seating capacity is unknown, but most historians agree on an estimate of about fifty thousand.

A reconstruction of the mighty "Amphitheater of the Flavians," or Colosseum, as it appeared in its heyday.

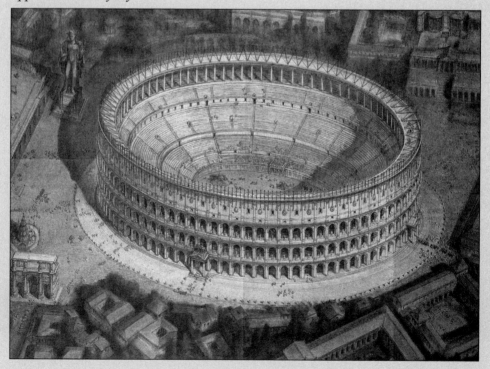

other kinds and pairings. One unusual gladiator about which little is known was the *provocator,* who was more heavily armored than the others and apparently fought only other *provocatores.* "They fought with the *scutum* . . . a *gladius* or other short sword . . . [and] wore normal armor on the sword arm and shield leg," Graham Ashford says of the *provocatores.*

> Their helmets and chest armor, though, is what makes them quite unique. Originally the helmets they wore took the Gallic style worn by contemporary Roman soldiers. In time, this helmet changed considerably to a large dome shape with heavy neck flares. . . . Covering the top portion of their chest they wore a piece of armor which sometimes managed to cover the top of the shoulders at least past the clavicle [collarbone]. . . . The armor would have been fixed by a leather cross piece . . . [that passed] from the sides of the armor piece and onto an iron ring placed in between the shoulder blades. In no depictions (I am aware of) do the *provocatores* fight anyone but their own type. This may be due to the light chest armor they are depicted wearing, which may well have given them too great an advantage over their opponent. . . . Little else is known of the provocator.[29]

Even more offbeat was the *dimachaerius,* an arena fighter who had no shield and fought with two swords (or daggers), one in each hand. Very few literary or artistic references to this gladiator have been found, so it is difficult to know exactly how he managed to face down more heavily armed opponents. Based on modern reconstructions of gladiatorial bouts staged by Ashford and other researchers, however, it appears that the *dimachaerius* attempted to confuse an adversary with a series of rapid slashes and thrusts of his blades. Eventually, the opponent might become flustered and make a mistake, at which point the *dimachaerius* likely jumped forward and delivered a fatal blow.

If these double-sword wielders were unusual, another unconventional group of gladiators, the *andabates,* were downright bizarre. The *andabates* fought while literally blindfolded by massive helmets with no eyeholes. Fortunately for these fighters, they wore coats of protective armor made of small iron rings or scales, so if one man was struck by an opponent's lucky blow, it might glance off and not cause serious damage. But how did a blind combatant mount an offensive? "In order to deceive his adversary," Auguet hypothesizes,

> the *andabate* might well maneuver in the arena with all the precautions of a skin-diver in deep water

anxious not to scare the fish; but it was not trickery any more than luck, but skill in swordsmanship and strength which were finally the decisive factors of victory, since the sole method of winning was to strike at the joints of the [armor].[30]

Thus, perhaps such a fighter learned to estimate the height and position of an opponent's weak points and then strike at them, hoping to do some damage.

Another unique gladiator type used the lasso (a rope with a slipknot in it, like that wielded by modern rodeo riders) as his main offensive weapon. Called the *laquearius,* evidently he first tried to trip or entangle his opponent in the lasso. Then the *laquearius* either choked the other person or stabbed him with a dagger.

MOUNTED GLADIATORS

Another lasso-throwing gladiator was the *equite,* who fought on horseback. Depictions in ancient art indicate that he also used a lance and a sword, although exactly how is unknown. Related to the *equites* were other mounted gladiators—the *essedarii*—who fought from moving chariots. This was almost certainly a Celtic style of fighting, as Julius Caesar described it in the journals he kept during his conquest of Gaul during the 50s B.C. (The Celts inhabited some of the lands north of the Alps and Danube River as well as Britain and Ireland.

Gauls were Celts living in what is now France.)

Occasionally, ancient literary works mentioned gladiator charioteers. For example, the first-century A.D. Roman novelist Petronius described an *essedarius,* who happened to be a woman, in his *Satyricon.* "We'll be having a holiday with a three-day show that's the best ever," says one of the characters in reference to an upcoming gladiatorial show,

> and not just a hack troupe of [slave] gladiators but freedmen. [The sponsor of the games] will give us cold steel, no quarter [i.e., no mercy for fallen fighters], and the slaughterhouse right in the middle [of the amphitheater]. . . . He's got some big brutes already, and a woman who fights in a chariot.[31]

Short passages mentioning gladiator charioteers also occur in the works of the first-century A.D. Roman humorist Martial.

On the other hand, some modern scholars disagree that the *essedarii* were full-fledged gladiators who fought in the *munera* proper. In their view, the mounted warriors mentioned by Petronius and Martial were more likely animal fighters and therefore low-level gladiators. If so, they were featured players in the wild beast shows that took place before the main gladiatorial combats.

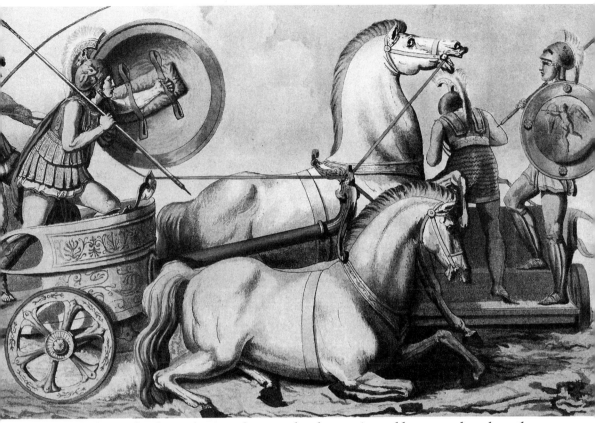

Some gladiators fought on chariots. One popular theme, pictured here, may have been the warrior-heroes of Homer's Iliad.

TEAM FIGHTERS AND RETIREES

Other offbeat and minor kinds of gladiators are mentioned in inscriptions. But nearly nothing is known about them except for their names. There were, in addition, a few more general designations for gladiators, but these were not based on their weapons, armor, and fighting styles but rather on how they were paired or on other factors. Most of the time gladiators fought in pairs, one-on-one, for example. No matter what their spe-

cific types (Samnite, *retiarius,* Thracian, *equite,* and so forth), these fighters were collectively called *ordinarii,* or "ordinary gladiators."

By contrast, once in a while larger numbers of gladiators fought, most often grouped into opposing teams. These combatants were collectively referred to as *catervarii,* meaning "group fighters" (or *gregatim,* meaning "in herds" or "in crowds"). Such large-scale combats could get out of hand more easily than regular two-person pairings. According to Suetonius in his biography of Caligula, that emperor was watching a group fight between a team of five *retiarii* and a team of five *secutores*. The net-men put on a poor performance, so Caligula ordered that they be executed for laziness. But suddenly, spurred to action by his plight, one *retiarius*

> seized a trident and killed each of the victorious team [of *secutores*] in turn. [The emperor] then publicly expressed his horror at what he called "this most bloody murder," and his disgust with those who had been able to stomach the fight. [32]

This real event was the partial inspiration for the exciting scene in the 1954 film *Demetrius and the Gladiators* in which the title character single-handedly slays several opponents in front of Caligula.

Another general designation of gladiators that applied regardless of their

War prisoners reenact a battle from earlier Roman history in an arena scene from Barabbas.

ROMAN GLADIATORS VS. GREEK ATHLETES

The Romans' fascination for gladiators was matched by their general disdain for Greek athletes, who mainly took part in Olympic-style events such as running, jumping, discus throwing, and wrestling. Boxing and chariot racing are the only Greek sports the Romans really enjoyed, and the Roman versions were considerably more vigorous and bloody. One reason for the Romans' dislike of Greek sports was the Greek custom of competing in the nude. Most Romans saw this as unmanly and immoral. Another major difference between Roman games and Greek sports was the degree of citizen participation. In Rome, gladiatorial and wild beast shows were popular as entertainment. But for a Roman citizen actually to participate in such public spectacles was seen as improper and socially unacceptable. In contrast, Greek society encouraged and glorified athletic participation by citizens.

types was *rudiarii*. These were fighters of all kinds who managed to survive the arena long enough to gain their freedom and retire. The name came from the *rudis,* the wooden sword they had trained with in the *ludus;* the *editor* awarded a *rudiarius* such a weapon as a ceremonial gift after the fighter's last public match.

Such veterans were almost always excellent and popular fighters, and many spectators were reluctant to see them go. Therefore, it was not unusual for games officials to offer large sums of money to lure *rudiarii* back into the arena for brief comebacks that pleased the crowds. According to Suetonius, the second emperor, Tiberius, "persuaded some retired gladiators to appear with the rest, by paying them 1,000 gold pieces each."[33] The highly applauded return of a *rudiarius* demonstrated that, no matter which weapons and style a gladiator employed in his work, winning was all that counted in the end.

CHAPTER 5

MORTAL COMBAT: PEOPLE VS. PEOPLE

After the *editor,* emperor, or other high official had inspected the gladiators' weapons and signified his approval, all of the fighters promptly left the arena, except for the pair previously selected for the first combat. Unfortunately, no detailed description of how they fought has survived. Indeed, ancient literary descriptions of gladiators in action are few, short, and superficial. So for the most part, their exact strategies and tactics in the arena remain uncertain.

In an effort to fill this void in the historical record, one cannot simply assume that gladiators used the same fighting style as Roman soldiers, whose tactics are much better documented. In fact, an often-cited account of an army battle by the fourth-century Roman historian Ammianus Marcellinus describes soldiers using a gladiator-like tactic; and the wording of the passage implies that this was not normal procedure for the soldiers. During this bat-

tle, the Roman troops fought against a group of German "barbarians." The Roman troops were on the defensive, huddled tightly in close quarters as the enemy attacked in a frenzy. "Our troops . . . stood firm as towers," Ammianus writes, "and renewed the battle with increased spirit. Taking care to avoid being wounded and covering themselves like gladiators, they plunged their swords into the barbarians' sides, which their wild rage left exposed." [34]

The vagueness of the phrase "covering themselves like gladiators" leaves the reader in the dark about the actual defensive move executed. But this has not stopped modern scholars from making educated guesses. For example, Roland Auguet suggests, "Perhaps one of the classic figures of this defensive technique consisted in placing one knee on the ground and watching, from behind the shield, for the first mistake on the part of the adversary." [35]

Partially making up for the general lack of ancient literary descriptions of actual gladiatorial fights are depictions of these combats in paintings, sculptures, and mosaics. The fighters in these renderings are static, of course. But the artists did manage to capture some of the basic postures of the combatants, including what modern scholars call the classic stance. Based in part on the ancient artistic depictions and also on modern reenactments of gladiatorial combats, scholars have managed to reconstruct a fairly plausible picture of what some of these bouts looked like. Also, certain clues in the historical record give an idea of the various possible outcomes of the matches—wins, losses, draws, appeals for mercy, executions, and so forth.

Nineteenth-century French artist Jean Gerome titled this painting Myrmillo, *but more recent scholarship suggests the fighter is a* hoplomachus.

DEFENSE, ATTACK, AND MORE DEFENSE

One major key to winning a gladiatorial match, modern reenactors have discovered, was not to panic and lose the high degree of protection provided by the classic defensive stance. Recall that in this posture, which the fighters had mastered in the *ludus,* they held their shields close to their bodies. Each distributed his weight evenly on both legs while planting the right leg farther back than the left. The sword or other weapon was kept behind the shield so that the opponent could not see it and guess at how it might strike at him. It was customary to hold this posture while sparring, or moving carefully around the opponent while constantly looking for weak points to exploit.

Sooner or later, one fighter felt he had found such a weak point, perhaps on one of the opponent's flanks (sides) or under his shield. When he judged the time was right, the attacker took a few short, quick steps forward toward the enemy. It was at this point, called the "breaking of the fight," that the attacker was most vulnerable because he momentarily had to abandon the protection ensured by the classic stance. As Graham Ashford points out, "Breaking the fight [was] often difficult and perilous as the attacker [had] to make a dangerous move by exposing his sword arm to attack."[36]

For the attacker's adversary, by contrast, the worst thing to do at this point was to panic and lower his guard by abandoning the classic stance. That would only further expose the weak point on his side or under his shield and help the attacker exploit it. "In most [ancient artistic] images left us where a contest has been broken," Ashford writes,

> it is normally because someone has managed to get around the side, back, or underneath the shield. It is this "breaking of the fight" that the classic stance is designed to limit by giving maximum protection behind the shield to the user, not just to the immediate front but also to his flanks. . . . The most common mistake . . . [was] to back out of the shield's protection when the other person [closed] threateningly. . . . By being correctly positioned within the [protective curve of the] shield, attacks from the side . . . [could] be easily avoided, as the side of the shield pushed the blade past the back and sides or in the worst case relegated a potentially lethal blow to a painful one. . . . In many [ancient painted and sculpted] gladiatorial images, the fight is all but lost because of the incorrect position of the [shield], which has left a side or arm uncovered. Wounds to these locations often resulted in the eventual defeat of the injured gladiator as exhaustion [was] quick to follow.[37]

Based on such reconstructions, many gladiatorial bouts must have been less displays of swordsmanship and more contests to see which fighter used his shield and defensive stance most judiciously. Even one simple mistake could lead to disaster. As Ashford points out, if one gladiator inflicted a wound on the other, the injured person could no longer perform at 100 percent capacity; unless he could score a lucky hit himself, the wounded individual was bound to tire rapidly, which worked to his opponent's advantage.

Obvious exceptions to this reliance on the shield's protection were fights in which one or both of the combatants had no shields. In such cases, a weapon held so that it pointed directly at the opponent and protected the user probably substituted for a shield. For example, when sparring, the *retiarius* likely led with his left leg and projected his trident forward with his left hand, while holding his net low in the right rear, ready to toss it when an opening presented itself. Similarly, the sparring *dimachaerius* may have held one of his swords forward with his left hand and kept the other blade low in his right hand in the back. Only when he leapt forward to attack would the rear sword come into play. Thus, even fighters without shields adopted a variation of the classic stance.

WIN, LOSE, OR DRAW

During these moments of sparring, attack, defense, and in some cases suc-

A retiarius *tosses his net at a charging* myrmillo, *who tries to counter it.*

cessful strikes, the gladiators had to contend with the constant distraction of the crowd's reactions. These were surely no less boisterous than those of the fans at modern boxing and wrestling matches. Spectators in the amphitheaters loudly urged on their favorites and booed and heckled others. Common Latin words and phrases heard during the *munera* included *"Verbera!"* ("Strike!"), *"Habet!"*

("A hit!"), *"Hoc habet!"* ("Now he's done for!"), *"Ure!"* ("Burn him up!"), and *"Jugula!"* ("Cut his throat!").

The matches these spectators watched had a number of different possible outcomes. The most common were recorded in lists compiled and distributed at the close of each *munus,* some of which have survived. Each list mentioned the fighters' names, followed by uppercase letters denoting the outcomes of the bouts. The letter P, for instance, stood for *periit,* meaning "perished"; V denoted *vicit,* or "won"; and M stood for *missus,* which indicated a fighter who lost but fought so well that he was allowed to live. Thus, not all matches ended in the death of one of the contestants.

A fourth possible outcome of a gladiatorial bout was known as *stans missus.* In this case, both combatants fought well and neither was able to beat the other decisively, so the *editor* called the match a draw. This was apparently a fairly common outcome because it was described frequently in ancient inscriptions. The epitaph of a gladiator named Flamma, for example, stated that in the course of thirty-eight matches he won twenty-five times, was *missus* four times, and *stans missus* nine times. If a fight ended in *stans missus,* any prizes, which could take the form of money, palm branches, or other items, were awarded to both or neither of the gladiators, depending on the situation. In one of his epigrams (short, often witty poems), Martial recorded the case of a draw in which the fighters, named Priscus and Verus, each received a prize:

An end to the even strife was found. Equal they fought, equal they yielded. To both, [the emperor, Domitian] sent wooden swords [symbolizing their discharge from the gladiatorial profession] and to both [victory] palms. Thus valor and skill had their reward. This has happened under no prince but you, [Domitian]: two fought and both won.[38]

THE FATE OF SLACKERS, LOSERS, AND COWARDS

Unfortunately for the gladiators, draws were not always allowed in the arena. Among the other possible outcomes of the bouts was the *sine missione,* in which the contestants had to keep fighting, no matter how long it took, until one was dead. Viewing this practice as unnecessarily cruel, the first emperor, Augustus, prohibited it. However, a number of his successors, especially those with reputations for insensitivity, like Caligula and Commodus, ignored the ban.

Still another fairly common occurrence in arena bouts was when both the presiding official and the audience felt that the gladiators were not putting enough energy and heart into the fight. The Romans would not tolerate lazy fighters, and the gladiator who did not give it his all in the arena risked a public call for him to be beaten or even executed. A character in Petronius's *Satyricon* expressed the prevailing attitude about lazy and otherwise substandard gladiators in some disparaging remarks about a politician who had sponsored a *munus:*

He put on some half-pint gladiators, so done-in already that they'd have dropped if you blew on them. I've seen animal killers [most of whom had less training than gladiators] fight better. . . . One boy did

This painting depicts a retiarius *slaying his opponent in a* sine missione *contest. Such bouts required contestants to fight to the death.*

SENECA'S DISDAIN FOR ARENA EXECUTIONS

The first-century A.D. *Roman playwright Seneca the Younger disliked at least some aspects of the killing that went on in amphitheaters. That much is clear from a passage (quoted in Moses Hadas's* The Stoic Philosophy of Seneca*) he wrote after witnessing the execution of a group of unarmed condemned men:*

I happened on the noon interlude at the arena, expecting some clever burlesque, some relaxation to give the spectators a respite [break] from human gore. [But] the show was the reverse. The fighting that had gone before [i.e., the regular gladiatorial fights] was charity by contrast. Now there was no nonsense about it; it was pure murder. The men have nothing to protect them; the whole body is exposed and every stroke tells. . . . There is no helmet or shield to parry the steel. Why armor? Why skill? Such things [merely] delay the [inevitable] kill.

have a little spirit—he was in Thracian armor, and even he didn't show any initiative. In fact, they were all flogged afterwards [for failing to fight well], there were so many shouts of "Give 'em what for!" from the crowd. Pure yellow [cowardice], that's all. [39]

Once in a while, an amphitheater audience witnessed what it viewed as an even more shocking and dishonorable display—when one of the fighters simply turned and ran for his life. How often this occurred is unknown. What is more certain is that the offender swiftly suffered a severe lashing with a whip, a branding with a hot iron, or death at the hands of his opponent. Alan Baker describes the most common way that one gladiator executed another: "The defeated gladiator would kneel on the ground facing the victor, and would clasp his thigh. The victorious gladiator would then hold the head of his opponent in his left hand and with his right plunge his sword into his neck." [40]

Escaping this grisly fate was certainly on the mind of any gladiator who was wounded during a bout, which was a common occurrence. The fallen fighter was permitted to raise one finger, essentially an appeal for mercy, and was expected to remain otherwise completely still while awaiting news of his fate. The vast majority of fallen, wounded gladiators showed incredible discipline and courage by quietly submitting themselves to the power of the onlookers.

The *editor,* emperor, or other high official present exercised this power, often according to the audience's wishes. For a long time, the traditional consensus among modern scholars was that if the spectators desired a fighter spared, they signaled their desire with a "thumbs-up" gesture; whereas if their choice was death, they indicated it with a "thumbs-down." This may indeed be what happened. However, several experts have offered other intriguing possibilities. One is a "thumbs-down," along with the waving of handkerchiefs, as the signal for the victor to drop his sword and spare the loser. Another consists of pressing the thumb toward the chest, symbolizing a sword through the heart, to call for the fallen fighter's death.

Although a fallen gladiator might escape death if the games officials

At the conclusion of a bout, spectators indicate that they want death for the fallen fighters in Jean Gerome's masterpiece, Police Verso *("Thumbs Down").*

WHY CHRISTIANS WERE CONDEMNED TO THE ARENA

Among the people who were executed in Roman amphitheaters were an unknown number of Christians. However, the popular notion that the Romans were religiously intolerant and persecuted the Christians for having different beliefs is mistaken. The Romans were highly tolerant of others' beliefs and themselves practiced numerous alternative and often exotic religions from around the Mediterranean world. What made the early Christians different was that they condemned all other beliefs but their own and often refused to acknowledge the emperor's divinity. Moreover, they kept to themselves, appearing to be antisocial. Over time, therefore, most people came to assume that the Christians were anarchists who hated the human race and wanted to destroy society. Worst of all, unfounded rumors spread that Christian rituals included cannibalism, incest, and other repugnant acts. Most Romans came to believe these fables and therefore felt little or no pity for the Christians who were executed in the arena.

A group of condemned Christians await a grisly fate in the Colosseum in this reconstruction.

and crowd were in a charitable mood, his chances of surviving by playing dead were pretty much nil. The authorities were prepared for such fakers. At the end of each bout, men dressed as ancient gods or demons ran out and applied red-hot irons to the body or bodies. And any pretender who cried out was swiftly dispatched to the Underworld by having his throat cut.

EXECUTIONS: ALL IN A DAY'S WORK

As part of the job, a gladiator was expected not only to kill one or more fellow gladiators but also to perform public executions of ordinary persons who had been convicted of crimes. These killings were not fair fights like the formal matches of the *munera*. Instead, they were out-and-out massacres since the condemned individuals were completely or almost completely defenseless. Thus, although such executions took place in the amphitheater on the same day as a gladiatorial display, they were not part of the *munus* proper.

Ironically, it was a mere twist of fate, fortunate for one person and sad for the other, that separated a gladiator from the criminal he was ordered to execute in the arena. A gladiator often started out as a criminal who had been condemned to train in a *ludus*, whereas another criminal might be sentenced to outright death

in the arena. The latter was said to be *noxii ad gladium ludi damnati,* or "condemned to be killed by the sword in the games." The court transferred such an unfortunate individual directly to the custody of the *editor,* who assured that the condemned would be dead within a year.

Most such executions took place around noon, shortly before the formal gladiatorial bouts began. Guards led the unarmed criminals up onto the arena floor, where several fully armed gladiators slaughtered some of them. Depending on the severity of the crimes they had committed, other prisoners were crucified. The worst offenders of all were tied to stakes, to be mauled and eaten by half-starved lions, bears, and other beasts. While these killings took place, attendants veiled any emperors' statues standing on pedestals around the arena, an effort to spare the high and mighty the sight of undignified "refuse" twisting in the agony of death. (According to one ancient account, the emperor Claudius ordered so many such executions that he had a statue of Augustus removed from the arena so it would not have to be perpetually veiled.)

As for how the gladiators who took part in these executions felt about their role in them, the ancient sources are mute. No such testimony by arena fighters, if it ever existed in the first place, has survived. It is likely that many gladiators had by this

GLADIATORS BOTH GLORIFIED AND DEGRADED

The societal double standard about gladiators was troublesome to some Romans, including the Christian apologist Tertullian, who wrote these words (quoted in Carlin A. Barton's The Sorrow of the Ancient Romans *) in the early third century.*

Men give them [gladiators] their souls, women their bodies too. On one and the same account, they glorify them and degrade and diminish them—indeed, they openly condemn them to ignominy [dishonor and humiliation] and the loss of civil rights, excluding them from the Senate House and rostrum [speaker's platform] . . . and all other honors or distinctions of any type. The perversity of it! Yet, they love whom they punish; they belittle whom they esteem; the art they glorify, the artist they debase. What judgment is this? On account of that for which he is vilified [condemned], he [the gladiator] is deemed worthy of merit!

time become so accustomed to the brutality of the arena that they saw the killing of criminals as simply all in a day's work. A few trained fighters may well have been repulsed by slaying unarmed people. But though they regretted it, they dared not protest or refuse; the penalty was for they themselves to join the ranks of the condemned and suffer their terrible fate.

CHAPTER 6

MORTAL COMBAT: PEOPLE VS. ANIMALS

Gladiators—that is, trained warriors whose work consisted of fighting one another to the death in amphitheaters—were not the only kind of Roman arena fighters. There were also their close professional kin—the *venatores,* meaning "hunters." The so-called hunts in which they participated were called *venationes.* "So-called" is used to emphasize that the term "hunt," as applied in the ancient Roman games, can be misleading. The *venatores* were not sportsmen stalking wild beasts in their natural habitats; rather, they were trained killers whose jobs consisted of confronting and slaughtering animals that had already been trapped and had no chance of escape. Some of the hunters also had the task of training and prodding animals to fight one another or to kill and eat condemned prisoners.

At first, the wild beast shows in which the hunters plied their grisly trade were minor spectacles presented mainly on the morning prior to the *munera* proper. The stands were not always full because in the morning a majority of Romans were busy working or taking care of personal affairs. However, the *venationes,* which were at first privately sponsored like the early gladiatorial bouts, steadily grew in popularity. By the late Republic and early Empire, the larger-scale *venationes* were not only run by the government but also were presented in the afternoon and attracted large crowds. On occasion, a hunt featured so many animal fights and executions that it went on for several days. Eventually there was a big and continuing public demand for the *venatores.*

THE HUNTERS' STATUS AND ARMOR

To be more precise, not all of the arena hunters were called *venatores.* Some

An arena hunter confronts a lioness in this fragment of a Roman fresco. Wearing no armor, the job of such hunters was very dangerous.

bore the name *bestiarii,* literally translated as "beast-men." By the second century A.D., the two labels may have become more or less interchangeable. Still, for a long time there was apparently a marked distinction between a *venator* and a *bestiarius.* A *venator* seems to have been a full-fledged hunter, who was superior in skill, status, and seniority to a *bestiarius.*

The term *bestiarius* was evidently long used to describe a number of different minor participants in the arena hunts, including those who assisted the *venatores* in various ways. It seems probable, for example, that a *bestiarius* was

a lower-level hunter who drove and prodded animals into position for the more expert *venatores,* who then fought and killed the beasts. A modern analogy would be the mounted picadors who use lances to herd and prepare bulls for Spanish matadors (bullfighters). A *bestiarius* may also have been a second-string hunter who assisted and followed the orders of a *venator* in confrontations with multiple animals. Criminals and other people condemned to be killed by beasts in the arena were also known as *bestiarii;* this may have derived from their close interaction with the lower-status hunters of the same name who tied them to stakes and encouraged beasts to attack them.

Although the exact terminology used to describe the various arena hunters remains somewhat uncertain, there is no question that they, at least the higher status ones, resembled gladiators in many ways. Like gladiators, most *venatores* began as slaves and criminals and, starting in the late first century B.C., trained in an imperial *ludus.* One major difference between the training regimens of the two kinds of fight-ers is that the hunters may have been less comprehensive and rigorous, although this is by no means certain. That arena hunters closely resembled gladiators or were viewed as lower-level gladiators is also confirmed by the similarity of their costumes. The out-fits donned by the hunters did change over time, but as late as the early Empire the two kinds of fighters were hard to tell apart. Relief sculptures of the first half of the first century A.D., historian Marcus Junkelmann points

The scene on this terra-cotta bas-relief from the first or second century A.D. seems to show a bestiarius *driving a lion toward a* venator.

out, "show *venatores* appearing in the [arena] with armaments—metal helmets, loincloths, greaves, swords . . . exactly like those of contemporary gladiators."[41]

By the later years of the first century, however, the arena hunters had become much less heavily armored. They wore only a plain tunic and some thick cloth leg wrappings. Also, their standard weapon was now the *venabulum,* a spear with an iron-reinforced point, with which they fought deer, ostriches, boars, and other creatures while either on foot or on horses. For a while, in the second century, the trend reversed as the *venatores* returned to more protective armor, including a broad belt that covered the abdomen and a small, decorated breastplate. But in the third century, the standard style once more reverted to simple tunics.

SPECIALISTS AND CROWD PLEASERS

It is important to emphasize that these hunters could vary considerably in their weaponry and fighting styles, just as gladiators did. Although the hunter who chased down and used his spear to dispatch beasts was perhaps the most prevalent type of *venator,* a number of specialists existed. Some wielded swords, daggers, clubs, or bows and arrows in addition to or instead of the spear. Those hunters who specialized in killing with the bow, for instance, were called *sagittarii.*

There were also specialized hunters called *taurarii* (or *taurocentae*), who squared off with bulls and tried to stab them with lances, much like modern matadors. (In fact, modern bullfights evolved over the centuries in Spain from Roman versions held there when it was part of the Roman Empire.) An exciting variation of the heavily armed Roman bullfighter is described here by Roland Auguet:

> The man, who had no weapon other than his muscles, [and was] mounted on horseback, closely raced the bull at full gallop to wear it down. At a suitable moment, he urged his horse forward and, at full gallop, leapt onto the neck of his adversary; he held on astride and then tried, by throwing his arms around the beast's horns . . . to throw it by twisting its neck.[42]

Except for the hunter's costume, this feat was evidently quite similar to one of the more popular events in modern rodeos.

In addition to employing varied styles like gladiators did, some of the arena hunters enjoyed almost as much fan adulation and allegiance as gladiators. One of the most popular of all the *venatores* mentioned in ancient writings was Carpophorus, who flourished during the reign of Domitian. Martial wrote three separate praises of this fighter, including this one:

❧ PROTECTION FOR THE SPECTATORS ❧

To make sure that wild beasts did not injure the spectators, the government enacted security measures, summarized here by former Oxford University scholar J.P.V.D. Balsdon (in his Life and Leisure in Ancient Rome *):*

When Caesar gave his great hunting games in the Circus Maximus in 46 B.C., a canal ten feet wide and ten feet deep was constructed, separating the audience from the arena. . . . The measures taken in Nero's amphitheater . . . were copied later in the Colosseum. The platform (*podium*) which surrounded the arena of the Colosseum, and above which the spectators' seats rose, was thirteen feet above ground level. At ground level between it and the arena itself was a wooden barricade from which at regular levels rose the tall masts for the awning. On these masts at a certain height were fixed elephant tusks, from which strong [protective] netting hung.

This scene from the 1922 Italian film Messalina *shows a raised platform and masts holding netting to protect the spectators.*

He plunged his spear also in a charging bear, once prime in the peak of the Arctic pole [possibly a reference to a polar bear]; he laid low a lion of unprecedented size, a sight to see, who might have done honor to Hercules' hands. [The mythical strongman Hercules was credited with slaying the powerful Nemean lion]. He stretched dead a fleet leopard with a wound felt from afar.[43]

Hunters like Carpophorus not only provided first-rate entertainment for the spectators but also, probably unwittingly, helped to strengthen an underlying political dimension promoted by the state. It was not unlike the situation in which gladiators dressed as defeated enemies to emphasize the superiority of Rome and its spirit. After conquering various lands and territories, the Romans began importing creatures native to those regions for use in the arena hunts. And the people who attended the *venationes* came to associate the beasts they watched with the regions in which these animals were captured. This remained a powerful reminder that Rome had become undisputed master of those regions. The hunters and their prey "encouraged the spectators to associate military prowess and the geographic expansion of Roman influence with various animals from the distant realms subject to Roman

might," scholar Richard C. Beacham points out. "Through the display of such exotic booty, power was rendered both graphic and entertaining."[44]

APPALLING CARNAGE

This "booty" included all manner of creatures, among them elephants, lions, tigers, leopards, panthers, bears, deer, elks, hyenas, ostriches, hippopotamuses, rhinoceroses, giraffes, wild boars, wild donkeys, and wild horses. In addition to fighting expert arena hunters like the famous Carpophorus, these animals were herded and goaded by *bestiarii* to grapple with one another. Martial describes a contest between two big cats:

A tigress that tended to lick the hand of the fearless [hunter] fiercely tore a wild lion with rabid tooth; a novelty, unknown in any times. She dared do no such thing while she lived in the high forests, but since she has been among us she has gained ferocity.[45]

In another epigram, Martial recalls how a group of low-level hunters provoked a rhinoceros into attacking several other beasts:

While the trembling [hunters] were goading the rhinoceros and the great beast's anger was long [increasing], men were giving up hope [that it would fight]. But at length the fury we earlier knew returned. For with his double horn he tossed a heavy bear as a bull tosses dummies. . . . He lifted two steers with his mobile neck [and] to him yielded the fierce buffalo and bison. A lion fleeing before him ran headlong upon the spears. [46]

Another common practice was for some *bestiarii* to tie one end of a rope to the leg of an animal and the other end to the leg of a second beast; the men then used whips and torches to force the creatures to fight each other.

The number of animals the hunters butchered in a typical beast show is unknown. But the number killed during a few special and unusually large-scale games are documented and give some idea of the appalling carnage involved. When the emperor Titus (Domitian's brother) inaugurated the Colosseum in A.D. 80, some nine thousand animals met their doom. Another eleven thousand beasts were slaughtered in 107 in a series of games presented by the emperor Trajan. All told, the arena hunters must have killed many millions of animals during the roughly six centuries in which the *venationes* were held.

In this scene from a Roman mosaic found in North Africa, a bear and bull are tied together and hunters prod them to fight.

OBJECTIONS TO THE HUNTERS' METHODS

Although the vast majority of Romans thoroughly enjoyed the bloody work of the arena hunters, a few did not. One of these was the noted first-century B.C. orator Cicero. He asked, "What pleasure can a civilized man find when either a helpless human being is mangled by a very strong animal, or a magnificent animal is stabbed again and again with a hunting spear?"[47]

In particular, Cicero was bothered by the way the hunters treated elephants in the amphitheaters. In this regard he was not alone, for apparently a good many Romans felt a degree of respect and sympathy for these giant creatures that transcended their feelings for most other animals. In 55 B.C., after attending a wild beast show of several days' duration in which several elephants put up heroic struggles yet still died cruel deaths, Cicero wrote to a friend:

> The last day was the day for elephants. The mob of spectators was greatly impressed, but showed no real enjoyment. In fact, a certain sympathy arose for the elephants, and a feeling that there was a kind of affinity between that large animal and the human race.[48]

In his *Natural History,* Pliny the Elder went into more detail about the hunters' mistreatment of the elephants in the same beast show:

> One elephant put up a fantastic fight and, although its feet were badly wounded, crawled on its knees against the attacking bands [of hunters]. It snatched away their shields and hurled them into the

✦ THE NOBLE AND DILIGENT ELEPHANT ✦

Of all the animals that appeared in the Roman *venationes,* the audience favorite was the elephant. Several surviving Roman accounts describe its intelligence, nobility, and diligence in training. In one public show, a group of six male and six female pachyderms entered the arena, where tables had been set for dinner, and then reclined and ate and drank like humans. Other elephants danced and walked tightropes. Perhaps the most remarkable and moving of all Roman elephants was the creature described by the scholar Pliny the Elder in his *Natural History.* "It is a known fact," he wrote, "that one elephant, somewhat slow-witted in understanding orders, was often beaten with a lash and was discovered at night practicing what he had to do [the next day]."

Another North African mosaic shows a leopard attacking a bound prisoner. This was a common form of execution for the worst criminals.

air. . . . There was also an extraordinary incident with a second elephant when it was killed by a single blow: a javelin struck under its eye and penetrated the vital parts of its head. All the elephants *en masse* [in a group], tried to break out through the iron railings that enclosed them, much to the discomfiture of the spectators. . . . But when [the] elephants had given up hope of escape, they played on the sympathy of the crowd, entreating [pleading with] them with indescribable gestures. They moaned, as if wailing, and caused the spectators such distress that . . . they rose in a body, in tears, and heaped dire curses on Pompey [the sponsor of the games].[49]

ANIMAL EXECUTIONERS

One aspect of the arena hunter's work that rarely raised any objections was the part he played in arena executions. Although full-fledged gladiators killed many of the condemned, some of the most despised criminals, including army deserters, traitors, and Christians, often faced mutilation and death in the clutches of fearsome beasts. Typically, after guards delivered the bound prisoners into the arena, *bestiarii* used whips and swords to force the victims to parade around while the crowd heaped scorn on them. Then the hunters tied the condemned to posts and prodded lions, bears, and other animals to attack them.

Perhaps the most famous and gruesome of these executions was that of a notorious bandit named Laureolus, who died in the arena in late republican times. His punishment later became the subject of a short dramatic skit written by the popular first-century B.C. Roman poet Catullus. In about A.D. 30, this skit began to be presented from time to time in the arena during wild beast shows. At first, an actor merely impersonated Laureolus and any blood spilled was fake, but eventually the performance became increasingly realistic. Starting in Domitian's reign, at the end of the skit some armed *bestiarii* forced a condemned criminal to take the place of the actor playing the bandit. The hunters nailed this pseudo-Laureolus to a cross and then coaxed a half-starved bear to attack him. "Hanging on no sham cross," Martial wrote after witnessing this hideous spectacle, Laureolus's unfortunate substitute

gave his naked flesh to a Caledonian bear. His lacerated limbs lived on, dripping gore, and in all his body, body there was none [i.e., his body had lost its normal shape]. Finally he met with the punishment he deserved; the guilty wretch had plunged a sword into his father's throat or his master's, or in his madness had robbed a temple of its secret gold, or laid a cruel torch to Rome. The criminal had outdone the misdeeds of ancient story; in him, what had been a play became an execution. [50]

❦ ANDROCLES AND THE LION ❧

In this excerpt from his Attic Nights, Aulus Gellius *quotes the earlier Egyptian scholar Apion, who claimed to have witnessed an extraordinary incident involving a lion and a condemned prisoner in the arena.*

A battle with wild beasts on a grand scale was being exhibited to the people. . . . There were many savage wild beasts, brutes remarkable for their huge size. . . . But beyond all others did the vast size of the lions excite wonder, and one of these in particular surpassed all the rest because of the huge size of his body. . . . There was brought in . . . the slave of an ex-consul; the slave's name was Androcles. When that lion saw him from a distance he stopped short as if in amazement, and then approached the man slowly and quietly, as if he recognized him. Then, wagging his tail in a mild and caressing way, after the manner and fashion of fawning dogs, he came close to the man, who was now half dead from fright, and gently licked his feet and hands. . . . Then you might have seen man and lion exchange joyful greetings, as if they had recognized each other.

It is interesting to note that the hunters may not always have been successful in getting animals to maul those condemned to die in the arena. There is the famous story of Androcles and the lion, for instance. Supposedly, the lion that was chosen to kill the condemned Androcles suddenly recognized him as the man who had once removed a splinter from its paw; the creature licked Androcles rather than hurt him, and the sponsor of the games allowed both to go free.

This tale is probably based on a fable attributed to the sixth-century B.C. Greek storyteller Aesop. However, the second-century A.D. Latin writer Aulus Gellius insisted that his source, an Egyptian writer named Apion, had actually witnessed such an incident in Rome. Apion was a contemporary of Seneca in the prior century. And Seneca mentioned a similar event involving a *venator* and a lion: "I have seen a lion in the amphitheatre who recognized one of the [hunters], who once had been his keeper, and protected him against the attacks of the other animals."[51] It is probable that Apion heard about this incident with the hunter and lion secondhand and confused it with the Androcles fable. If Seneca's account was indeed based on fact, that brief moment of friendship between man and beast stood in stark and noble contrast to the arena hunter's usually bloody work.

CHAPTER 7

EMPERORS WHO FOUGHT IN THE ARENA

The gladiatorial profession required much intense and specialized training. And few Romans would dare to fight a gladiator, either in or outside of the arena. Yet now and then a few well-known amateurs attempted to do just that, mainly because they were fascinated by both the spectacle of the arena bouts and the heroic image enjoyed by winning gladiators. These famous amateurs were a handful of Roman emperors. They courted ridicule and scandal to be sure; after all, even though gladiators were applauded as heroes, society still looked on them as lowlifes. Indeed, as historian Alan Baker puts it, nowhere is the strange Roman double standard about arena fighters "more forcefully represented than in the habit of some emperors of actually entering the arena themselves and taking on the role of gladiator or [beast fighter]." [52]

It is only natural to wonder why the leader of the strongest empire on Earth,

someone who enjoyed unprecedented power and security, would risk bodily injury and a tarnished reputation to fight in the arena. First, at no time did the emperors in question put themselves at serious risk when facing gladiators or wild beasts. The emperors' opponents always labored at some initial disadvantage. Or armed guards oversaw the matches, ready to step in and save their bosses if they got into any trouble. As far as their reputations were concerned, most of these rulers cared little what the people thought of them. The most notorious of the emperors who fought in the arena—Commodus, Caligula, and Nero—were arrogant, self-centered, and brutal tyrants who were already infamous for committing all manner of outrageous acts. Their forays into the arena became a lurid but fascinating footnote to the already colorful and compelling profession of the gladiators and hunters.

DOMITIAN'S INTEREST IN GLADIATORS

It was this compelling allure of the arena that motivated these rulers to fight in public. In this regard, they were decidedly atypical. For most Romans, there was a definite line between having an intense interest in the arena and actually fighting in it. Indeed, a number of emperors were enthralled or even obsessed by gladiators, but they never crossed that line.

Domitian, another despot cut from the same cloth as Caligula and Nero, was a case in point. Domitian was a major fan of the *munera.* Not only did he enjoy watching women fight in the arena, he strongly favored a certain type of male gladiator—the *myrmillones* with their fish-crested Samnite helmets. At the same time, he hated Thracian gladiators, with their curved swords and small shields. Suetonius recorded an incident that demonstrates how seriously Domitian took the rivalry between these two kinds of fighters. One day when the emperor was in his royal box at the recently finished Colosseum, a *myrmillo* and a Thracian were engaged in combat. "A chance remark by one citizen," Suetonius recalls,

This drawing is based on a surviving statue of Domitian.

> to the effect that a Thracian gladiator might be "a match for his . . . opponent but not for the patron of the games [i.e., Domitian himself]," was enough to have him dragged from his seat and—with a placard tied around his neck reading: "A Thracian supporter who spoke disloyally"—torn to pieces by dogs in the arena.[53]

Domitian spent many long hours watching gladiators at work, sometimes even at night by torchlight. Yet he never seriously considered fighting one of them. "Domitian was such a prey to fear and anxiety that the least sign of danger unnerved him," Suetonius writes. He "hated to exert himself. While in Rome he hardly ever went for a walk, and . . . weapons did not interest him."[54]

CALIGULA'S LOVE FOR THRACIAN FIGHTERS

One of Domitian's predecessors, Caligula, did occasionally cross the line and enter the world of the arena fighters, even though he never faced the real

danger they did. The great-grandson of the first emperor, Augustus, Caligula at first gave every indication of becoming a mild-mannered and constructive ruler.

Not long after assuming the throne, however, Caligula suffered a bout of serious illness, which seems to have affected his mind. After his recovery he grew increasingly twisted and corrupt. According to Suetonius, he murdered and tortured many people and told his grandmother, "Bear in mind that I can treat anyone exactly as I please!"[55]

A gladiator is summoned before the demented Caligula (standing in front of the throne). Caligula loved Thracian fighters.

❧ THE MENTALLY UNBALANCED CALIGULA ❧

Gaius Caesar, better known to history as Caligula, was born in A.D. 12. The son of the noted general Germanicus and his wife Agrippina the Elder, the boy accompanied his parents on campaigns and spent a number of years living in army camps. Caligula succeeded the second emperor, Tiberius, after the latter died in 37. The new ruler was at first popular with both the senators and the people. But soon he began displaying corrupt, mentally unbalanced be-havior, which grew worse as time progressed. Ignoring the public good, Caligula spent most of the state treasury on public games and personal luxuries; and to raise the money to continue his extravagant lifestyle, he imposed several heavy and unfair taxes. He also suggested that statues of himself should replace those of the god Jupiter in temples. Caligula became so hated that he was assassinated by his own bodyguards in January 41.

Other examples of Caligula's meanness and cruelty occurred at the public games:

> A crowd bursting into the Circus [Maximus, where chariot races were held] . . . to secure free seats angered him so much that he had them driven away with clubs. . . . During gladiatorial shows he would have the canopies removed [from the top of the facility] at the hottest time of the day and forbid anyone to leave; or [he would] . . . pit feeble old fighters against decrepit wild animals.[56]

Indeed, Caligula was just as fascinated by the *munera* and the wild beast shows as Domitian was. Caligula's preferences for specific types of gladiators was exactly the opposite of Domitian's, however. Whereas Domitian loved *myrmillones* and hated Thracians, Caligula adored Thracians and despised *myrmillones,* as well as *secutores,* who resembled the *myrmillones.* Caligula showed these biases by promoting the interests of Thracians and doing harm to their opponents. According to Suetonius:

> He chose Thracian gladiators to officer his German bodyguard. He reduced the defensive armor of the [*secutores*], and when a gladiator of this sort, called Columbus, won a fight but was slightly wounded, Caligula had him treated with a virulent [potent] poison, which he afterwards called "Columbinum."[57]

Caligula reserved his most passionate hatred for the *myrmillones,* however. So much did he dislike them that apparently he felt he must have the satisfaction of killing one himself. One day the emperor sauntered into one of the imperial gladiator schools in the capital and demanded that he be allowed to fight a *myrmillo* in a sparring match with wooden swords. The gladiator he singled out evidently decided that his best course was to let Caligula win; hopefully the demented ruler would then be satisfied and leave. This turned out to be a mistake, though, since the emperor could not be satisfied with anything less than the other man's death. After the two had sparred for a while, Suetonius writes, the *myrmillo* "fell down deliberately." But to his surprise, Caligula suddenly "drew a real dagger, stabbed him to death, and ran about waving the palm-branch of victory." [58]

Caligula also fought a number of times in the public arena, where, not surprisingly, he was always arrayed as a Thracian. Still, he wore little or no armor since he was well guarded and his opponents did not dare attempt to harm him. To the audiences who watched, these bouts must have appeared merely ceremonial in nature, whereas the emperor likely fancied that he was actually defeating his adversaries.

Nero and the Lion

Eventually, Caligula died the kind of death merited by his cruel and infamous deeds. In A.D. 41, members of his own imperial bodyguard stabbed him to death. One of his immediate successors,

Nero (who reigned from 51 to 68), apparently learned nothing from the lesson of Caligula's misrule and violent death. Nero was a self-centered, extravagant, and often cruel individual who fancied himself a brilliant musician, actor, and athlete. In reality, his efforts in all of these areas were mediocre at best. His harp playing and singing were so boring, for example, that some members of the captive audiences at his recitals pretended to faint so that attendants would carry them out.

As a would-be athlete, Nero most enjoyed driving chariots in public. At the Olympic Games in A.D. 68, the conceited ruler drove a chariot drawn by ten horses. "He fell from the chariot," Suetonius recalls, "and had to be helped in again . . . [and] failed to stay the course and retired before the finish." [59] Despite this poor performance, the judges decided it was in their own best interest to award Nero the victor's prize.

Regarding the arena, Nero, who was fascinated by animals, was more interested in the beast shows than in the gladiatorial fights. He eventually got up enough nerve to make an appearance as a *venator.* He dressed up like the mythical hero Hercules, who was famous for slaying a fierce lion. The vain Nero was not about to risk his skin, however; he made sure that the lion selected was docile and carefully trained not to attack a person. Under the watchful eye of his bodyguards, the emperor confronted the "savage" beast in the arena, and when the animal's attention strayed elsewhere, he swiftly used a club to crack its skull.

COMMODUS THE ARENA HUNTER

Another emperor fond of using clubs in the arena was Commodus, who, following the death of his father, Marcus Aurelius, in A.D. 180, ruled the Empire until 192. Like Caligula and Nero before him, Commodus was a vain, spendthrift, thoughtless, and brutal ruler. Also like his two notorious predecessors, Commodus saw himself as a valiant arena fighter. In fact, Commodus appeared

❧ COMMODUS: DESPOT AND GLADIATOR ☙

Born the son of the emperor Marcus Aurelius in A.D. 161, Commodus ascended the Roman throne in 180, at the age of nineteen. As a ruler, Commodus was a conceited and selfish despot, who neglected his responsibilities in favor of enjoying personal luxuries and pleasures. He saw himself as a great warrior and indulged this fantasy by appearing often in the arena (although always protected by guards). Unwilling to interrupt his comfortable lifestyle with time-consuming military campaigns, Commodus struck a deal with barbarian tribesmen who were then threatening the Empire; many were allowed to settle in the northern provinces, and about thirteen thousand of them joined the Roman army. Commodus also instituted a reign of terror in the capital, executing many prominent people on minor charges. Few were surprised or sorry when one of the several plots to assassinate him succeeded in 192.

Commodus's assassin, a wrestler, crouches over the emperor's lifeless body.

in public as either a *venator* or a gladiator more times than all of the other Roman emperors combined.

It is difficult to gauge the accuracy of the ancient accounts that describe Commodus's arena exploits. The various estimates for the numbers of animals and men he supposedly fought and killed run into the thousands; and they were likely based on government figures that had been purposely exaggerated to make him seem more formidable than he actually was. For example, the *Augustan History,* a fourth-century collection of imperial biographies compiled by an unknown Roman scholar, claimed that

> he [Commodus] killed with his own hand many thousands of wild animals, even elephants. . . . Such was his strength in slaying wild animals that he transfixed an elephant with a pole, pierced a wild goat's horn with a spear, and dispatched many thousands of huge beasts, each with a single blow.[60]

Even more incredible is the claim by Herodian, a third-century Syrian historian, that, among other notable feats, Commodus, slew a hundred lions with a hundred arrows:

> Everybody was amazed by the accuracy of his shooting. Using arrows with curved tips, he shot at [North African] ostriches, running as fast as their legs and flapping wings would carry them, and, the tops of their necks severed by the force of the blow, they went on running, though decapitated, as if nothing had happened. A leopard charged and got its teeth into the hunter who challenged it, and was on the point of

A bust of Commodus sporting the lion's skin and club of the hero Hercules.

❧ COMMODUS THE *VENATOR* ❧

The unknown fourth-century author of the Augustan History *wrote this about Commodus's exploits as an arena hunter:*

He killed with his own hand many thousands of wild animals, even elephants. Frequently it was before the eyes of the Roman people that he did these things. For such things as these, to be sure, he was strong enough, but otherwise he was weak and feeble, even having something wrong with him in the groin, which stuck out so much that the Roman people could detect the swelling through his silk clothing. . . . Such was his strength in slaying wild animals that he transfixed an elephant with a pole, pierced a wild goat's horn with a spear, and dispatched many thousands of huge beasts, each with a single blow.

This drawing is based on a statue of Commodus dressed in hunting attire.

mauling him when Commodus at the vital moment struck it with his spear, killing it and saving its victim. A hundred lions were released from below ground. With a hundred shots he killed them all and there they lay, all over the arena, and people had plenty of time to count them and see that not one single shot had failed to gain its mark. [61]

COMMODUS THE GLADIATOR

Commodus "also engaged in gladiatorial combat," says the author of the *Augustan History,* "and accepted a gladiator's name, with pleasure, as if he were accepting triumphal honors."[62] Among the gladiator names Commodus went by were Amazonius and Hercules. He was particularly enamored of Hercules, whose trademarks included a lion's skin and a club, and often adopted the legendary strongman's image. Hercules had never been as cruel and unjust as Commodus, however. One of the most infamous incidents of this pseudo-Hercules involved the merciless slaughter of a group of handicapped men. The second-century A.D. Roman historian Dio Cassius recorded it:

> Once, he got together all the men in the city who had lost their feet as the result of disease or some accident, and then, after . . . giving them sponges to throw instead of stones, killed them with blows of a club, pretending that they were giants.[63]

When engaged in the more usual single gladiatorial combats, Commodus most often fought as a *secutor.* According to the *Augustan History:*

> Commodus would take up the weapons of a gladiator as a "pursuer" [i.e., a *secutor*], covering his bare shoulders with a purple cloth. . . . Among his . . . triumphal titles he was called "First Stake [*primus palus,* or leader] of the Pursuers" six hundred and twenty times [one

time for each appearance as a *secutor*].[64]

It is important to emphasize that the emperor was never in any serious danger when facing trained fighters. Not only did Commodus have guards standing nearby to intervene if necessary, but his opponents were armed with wooden swords whereas he wielded real, lethal weapons.

THE GLADIATOR'S CORPSE

Commodus's despicable behavior, both inside and outside the arena, made him widely hated. And a palace plot to kill him eventually succeeded. The disdain the Roman people had for Commodus, as well as for the image of the gladiator, which he had embraced, was clearly expressed in a decree issued by the Senate directly following his assassination. It read, in part:

> Let the enemy of the fatherland . . . the gladiator, be mangled in the charnel-house [mortuary]! . . . Let the remembrance of . . . [Commodus] the gladiator be wiped out! Let the statues . . . [of him] be dragged down, let the remembrance of the foul gladiator be wiped out! . . . More savage than Domitian, more foul than Nero, as he did to others, let it be done to him! . . . Let the gladiator's corpse be dragged with the hook, let the gladiator's corpse be placed in the charnel-house![65]

A gladiator's corpse is dragged away by a hook, as described in the Senate's angrily-worded decree following Commodus's demise.

It is true that Roman crowds often cheered gladiators and made them heroes of the moment. But as Commodus learned the hard way, Roman society would not condone mixing the work of the gladiator with that of "decent" people, most especially the emperor. In the world of Rome, absolute power could and sometimes did corrupt absolutely. But there was always a stiff price to pay.

OUTLAWING THE PROFESSION

The Roman *munera* and *venationes* remained popular and kept the gladiators and arena hunters training and working during decade after decade, century after century. Yet these fighters and their combats were not destined to outlive the civilization that had spawned and nourished them. The last Roman emperor was forced from his throne in A.D. 476; and by the late 500s, the former Empire was a mere memory. The once grand city of Rome had shrunk to a near–ghost town of a few thousand inhabitants. At this point the Roman games no longer existed, and grass and bushes had begun to grow in the arenas and bleachers of the Colosseum and other amphitheaters.

THE CHRISTIANS VS. THE GLADIATORS

The first of the amphitheater attractions to go were the gladiatorial fights, mainly at the insistence of Roman Christians. They had first appeared in small numbers in the first century A.D. and for a long time had remained a widely hated minority in Roman society. Most Romans mistakenly thought the Christians were troublemakers, baby killers, and anarchists. So the Roman state periodically persecuted the Christians. Christian meeting-houses were burned, and an unknown number of Christians were condemned to die at the hands of gladiators and the claws of wild beasts in the arena.

The Christians were persistent, however, and their numbers slowly grew over the centuries. In the early fourth century, they received an important boost from the emperor Constantine I, who granted them religious toleration; he also helped them by converting to the faith on his deathbed. In the decades that followed, all but one of the emperors were Christians. And by the close of the century, Rome's government was firmly in the hands of Christians (though a majority of the Empire's inhabitants were still pagans, or non-Christians).

The political ascendancy of the Christians spelled the end of the gladiatorial combats. Christian leaders con-demned these fights as murder and an offense against humanity, frequently citing the words of an earlier Christian notable, Tertullian:

He who shudders at the body of a man who died by nature's law . . .

Christians are slaughtered in a Roman arena. Eventually, the Christians gained political power and banned gladiatorial bouts.

will, in the amphitheater, gaze down with most tolerant eyes on the bodies of men mangled, torn to pieces, defiled with their own blood; yes, and he who comes to the spectacle to signify his approval of murder being punished, will have a reluctant gladiator hounded on with lash and rod to do murder. [66]

That the gladiatorial profession promoted the merciless public slaughter of human beings was not the only objection raised against it by the Christians. Another reason Christian leaders wanted to ban these fights was, as Alan Baker points out, because they were

a form of resurrection that had nothing to do with the Christian god. In pagan Roman eyes, the gladiator (in spite of the adulation he received from the public) was *infamis* [disreputable or disgraced], occupying the very lowest level of society; and yet, by the nature of his profession, he was offered the chance of regaining his *virtus* [moral worth] by displaying skill and bravery in the arena. The salvation thus offered by gladiatorial combat was unacceptable to Christianity, since it was offered not by God, but by the Roman people. For this reason, as much as for the principle of Christian brotherly kindness, the practice of

gladiatorial combat could not continue. [67]

Thus, after taking control of the apparatus of Rome's government, Christian leaders continually denounced the *munera*. And by the end of the fourth century they had managed to close down the gladiator schools. Some gladiatorial bouts continued to be staged in the Colosseum and other amphitheaters from time to time for a few more years. But the numbers of trained fighters rapidly diminished as they died or retired. By 430 at the latest, their combats ceased and their profession disappeared.

ROME'S RAPID DECLINE

The Romans were not yet willing to give up the wild beast shows, however. The Colosseum and other amphitheaters still presented shows featuring animals, as well as public executions, for more than another century. Christian leaders evidently did not disapprove of these spectacles. As late as 523, large crowds still packed the amphitheaters to enjoy the *venationes*, and wrestling matches had become popular events, perhaps as tamer replacements for the prohibited gladiatorial combats.

This situation was bound to change, though, as the city of Rome had already begun its precipitous decline from the capital of the known world to a minor cultural backwater. Beginning in the late 520s, the city increasingly fell

Today, the Colosseum is a largely empty shell. The tiered stone seats are gone, along with the arena floor, where gladiators once fought and died.

into disrepair and its administrative and other services broke down. This forced more and more of its residents to leave and disperse into the countryside. Simply put, the complex and wealthy government that had long supported the public games and maintained the amphitheaters no longer existed; and massive crowds with plenty of leisure time to attend such events were also a thing of the past. Sometime in the mid–sixth century, the work of arena fighters, who had entertained millions of fans over the centuries, ended forever.

NOTES

INTRODUCTION: THE ORIGINS OF THE GLADIATORIAL PROFESSION

1. Michael Grant, *Gladiators.* New York: Delacorte, 1967, p. 30.
2. Livy, *History of Rome from Its Foundation,* excerpted in *Livy, Vol. 2,* trans. Canon Roberts. New York: E.P. Dutton, 1912, p. 125.
3. Suetonius, *Julius Caesar,* in *Lives of the Twelve Caesars,* published as *The Twelve Caesars,* trans. Robert Graves, rev. Michael Grant. New York: Penguin, 1979, p. 17.
4. Carlin A. Barton, *The Sorrow of the Ancient Romans: The Gladiator and the Monster.* Princeton, NJ: Princeton University Press, 1993, p. 35.

CHAPTER 1: HOW PEOPLE BECAME ARENA FIGHTERS

5. Alan Baker, *The Gladiator: The Secret History of Rome's Warrior Slaves.* New York: St. Martin's, 2000, pp. 21–22.
6. Quoted in Jo-Ann Shelton, ed., *As The Romans Did: A Sourcebook in Roman Social History.* New York: Oxford University Press, 1988, p. 345.
7. Juvenal, *Satires,* published as *Juvenal: The Sixteen Satires,* trans. Peter Green. New York: Penguin, 1974, p. 130.

8. Suetonius, *Domitian,* in *Twelve Caesars,* p. 301.
9. Graham Ashford, "Women Gladiators?" Ludus Gladiatorius, 2001. www.ludus.org.uk.
10. Juvenal, *Satires,* p. 136.
11. Calpurnius Flaccus, *Declamatio,* quoted in Barton, *Sorrow of the Ancient Romans,* p. 12.

CHAPTER 2: TRAINING FOR A DANGEROUS JOB

12. Grant, *Gladiators,* p. 40.
13. Seneca, *Moral Letters,* trans. Richard M. Gummere. London: William Heinemann, 1918, p. 52.
14. Plutarch, *Life of Crassus,* in *Parallel Lives,* excerpted in *Fall of the Roman Republic: Six Lives by Plutarch,* trans. Rex Warner. New York: Penguin Books, 1972, p. 122.
15. Graham Ashford, "The Classic Stance," Ludus Gladiatorius, 2002. www.ludus.org.uk.
16. Ashford, "The Classic Stance."

CHAPTER 3: THE ELABORATE PRESHOW CEREMONIES

17. Quoted in Shelton, *As the Romans Did,* p. 344.
18. Quoted in Shelton, *As the Romans Did,* p. 345.
19. Pliny the Elder, *Natural History,* excerpted in *Pliny the Elder: Natural*

History: A Selection, trans. John H. Healy. New York: Penguin, 1991, pp. 328–29.

20. Jerome Carcopino, *Daily Life in Ancient Rome: The People and the City at the Height of the Empire,* rev. ed. New Haven, CT: Yale University Press,1992, p. 239.
21. Suetonius, *Claudius,* in *Twelve Caesars,* p. 199.
22. Suetonius, *Caligula,* in *Twelve Caesars,* p. 167.
23. Roland Auguet, *Cruelty and Civilization: The Roman Games.* London: Routledge, 1994, p. 44.
24. Marcus Junkelmann, *"Familia Gladiatoria:* The Heroes of the Amphitheater,"* in Eckart Kohne, ed., *Gladiators and Caesars: The Power of Spectacle in Ancient Rome.* Berkeley and Los Angeles: University of California Press, 2000, p. 66.
25. Baker, *The Gladiator,* p. 184.

CHAPTER 4: DIFFERENT WEAPONS AND FIGHTING STYLES

26. Baker, *The Gladiator,* p. 55.
27. Stephen Wisdom, *Gladiators: 100 B.C.–A.D. 200.* Oxford, UK: Osprey, 2001, pp. 31–32.
28. Quoted in Auguet, *Cruelty and Civilization,* p. 80.
29. Graham Ashford, *"Provocator,"* Ludus Giadiatorius, 2001. www.ludus.org.
30. Auguet, *Cruelty and Civilization,* pp. 59–60.

31. Petronius, *The Satyricon,* trans. J.P. Sullivan. New York: Penguin Books, 1977, p. 59.
32. Suetonius, *Caligula,* in *Twelve Caesars,* p. 169.
33. Suetonius, *Tiberius,* in *Twelve Caesars,* p. 117.

CHAPTER 5: MORTAL COMBAT: PEOPLE VS. PEOPLE

34. Ammianus Marcellinus, *History,* published as *The Later Roman Empire, A.D. 354–378,* trans. and ed. Walter Hamilton. New York: Penguin, 1986, p. 113.
35. Auguet, *Cruelty and Civilization,* p. 80.
36. Ashford, "The Classic Stance."
37. Ashford, "The Classic Stance."
38. Martial, *Epigrams,* vol. 1, ed. and trans. D.R. Shackleton Bailey. Cambridge, MA: Harvard University Press, 1993, pp. 33–35.
39. Petronius, *Satyricon,* pp. 59–60.
40. Baker, *The Gladiator,* p. 85.

CHAPTER 6: MORTAL COMBAT: PEOPLE VS. ANIMALS

41. Junkelmann, *"Familia Gladiatoria,"* p. 71.
42. Auguet, *Cruelty and Civilization,* p. 91.
43. Martial, *Epigrams,* vol. 1, p. 25.
44. Richard C. Beacham, *Spectacle Entertainments of Early Imperial Rome.* New Haven, CT: Yale University Press, 1999, p. 12.
45. Martial, *Epigrams,* vol. 1, p. 27.

46. Martial, *Epigrams,* vol. 1, pp. 29–31.
47. Quoted in Shelton, *As the Romans Did,* p. 347.
48. Quoted in Shelton, *As the Romans Did,* p. 347.
49. Pliny the Elder, *Natural History,* pp. 111–12.
50. Martial, *Epigrams,* vol. 1, p. 19.
51. Seneca, *On Benefits,* trans. Aubrey Stewart. London: George Bell, 1887, p. 39.

CHAPTER 7: EMPERORS WHO FOUGHT IN THE ARENA
52. Baker, *The Gladiator,* p. 115.
53. Suetonius, *Domitian,* in *Twelve Caesars,* p. 306.
54. Suetonius, *Domitian,* in *Twelve Caesars,* pp. 309, 312.
55. Suetonius, *Caligula,* in *Twelve Caesars,* p. 168.
56. Suetonius, *Caligula,* in *Twelve Caesars,* p. 167.
57. Suetonius, *Caligula,* in *Twelve Caesars,* p. 181.
58. Suetonius, *Caligula,* in *Twelve Caesars,* p. 170.
59. Suetonius, *Nero,* in *Twelve Caesars,* p. 226.
60. *Augustan History,* published as *Lives of the Later Caesars, the First Part of the* Augustan History, *with Newly Compiled* Lives *of Nerva and Trajan,* trans. Anthony Birley. New York: Penguin, 1976, pp. 172–73.
61. Quoted in J.P.V.D. Balsdon, *Life and Leisure in Ancient Rome,* New York: McGraw-Hill, 1969, p. 310.
62. *Augustan History,* p. 171.
63. Quoted in Baker, *The Gladiator,* p. 124.
64. *Augustan History,* p. 174.
65. *Augustan History,* p. 177.

EPILOGUE: OUTLAWING THE PROFESSION
66. Tertullian, *Apology,* quoted in Peter Quennell, *The Colosseum.* New York: Newsweek Book Division, 1971, p. 75.
67. Baker, *The Gladiator,* p. 205.

GLOSSARY

amphitheater (in Latin, *amphitheatrum*, meaning "double theater"): A wooden or stone structure, usually oval shaped and open at the top, in which the ancient Romans staged public games and shows, including gladiatorial fights.

andabates: Gladiators who fought while blindfolded by helmets with no eyeholes.

bestiarius **(plural, *bestiarii*):** "Beastman"; an arena hunter who may have had a low status and assisted a *venator.*

catervarii: "Group fighters"; gladiators who fought in groups rather than pairs.

cena libera: The banquet attended by gladiators the night before their appearance in the arena.

dimachaerii: Gladiators who fought without shields and used two swords, one in each hand.

doctores: "Teachers"; trainers of gladiators and other arena fighters.

equites: Gladiators who fought on horseback.

essedarii: Gladiators who fought from moving chariots.

familia gladiatorum: "Family of gladiators"; the group of gladiators under the charge of a *lanista* or *procurator.*

gladiatrix: A women gladiator.

gladius: The sword wielded by Roman soldiers and several types of gladiators and the word from which "gladiator" was derived.

hoplomachus: A kind of gladiator who may have been intended to represent a hoplite (a Greek infantry soldier).

infamia: "Bad reputation"; a social stigma shared by Roman actors, gladiators, and other public performers.

lanista: A professional supplier of gladiators.

laquearii: Gladiators whose principal weapon was the lasso.

libellus munerarius: A written program listing the gladiators set to appear in an upcoming *munus.*

ludi **(singular, *ludus*):** Public games and shows in ancient Rome; also, schools where arena fighters trained.

Morituri te salutant!: "Those about to die salute you!"; the phrase recited by gladiators just prior to combat.

munera **(singular, *munus*):** "Offerings" or "duties"; public shows involving gladiators.

myrmillo **(or *murmillo*): "Fish-man"; a kind of gladiator, similar to a Samnite but with a crest of a fish on his helmet.**

noxii ad gladium ludi damnati: "Condemned to be killed by the sword in the games"; a death sentence to be carried out in the arena.

ordinarii: "Ordinary gladiators"; gladiators who fought in pairs.

paegniarii: Mock fighters who performed before the actual gladiatorial bouts.

palus: A six-foot-tall wooden pole used by gladiatorial trainees as a stand-in for an opponent.

parma: A small round or square shield used by Thracian warriors and gladiators.

pompa: The paradelike ceremony that opened gladiatorial fights, chariot races, and other spectacles.

primus palus: The most skilled and feared group of gladiators in a barracks; the *secundus palus* was the second best, and so on.

procurator: The manager of a gladiator school in imperial times.

provatio armorum: The inspection of gladiators' weapons just prior to combat.

retiarius (plural, *retiarii*): "Net-wielder"; a kind of gladiator who wore no armor and carried a net and a long trident.

rudis: A wooden sword used by training gladiators; the *rudis* was also a symbol of a retiring gladiator.

sagittarii: Arena fighters who used bows and arrows to slaughter animals.

Samnite: A member of a fierce central Italian hill tribe conquered by the Romans during the early Republic; or a kind of gladiator attired as a Samnite warrior—heavily armored and carrying a sword and heavy shield.

scutum: The rectangular shield carried by Roman soldiers and also by certain gladiators, including the *myrmillones* and the Samnites.

secutor: "Pursuer"; a kind of gladiator who was similar to a Samnite except that his helmet was more rounded and protective.

sica: A curved short sword wielded by Thracian warriors and gladiators.

sine missione: "To the death"; a kind of gladiatorial combat in which the combatants had to continue fighting until one was killed.

stans missus: The condition of a gladiator who attained a draw.

taurarii (or *taurocentae*): Arena fighters who specialized in fighting and killing bulls.

Thracians: Natives of the northern Greek region of Thrace; or gladiators attired as Thracian warriors—lightly armored and carrying a curved sword and small round shield.

venationes (singular, *venatio*): "Hunts"; various kinds of animal shows that took place in amphitheaters.

venator (plural, *venatores*): "Hunter"; an arena performer who fought and killed animals.

CHRONOLOGY

B.C.

753

The traditional date for the founding of Rome.

509

Rome's leading nobles depose their king and establish the Roman Republic.

264

The city of Rome witnesses its first gladiatorial combats, a private affair held at the funeral of a nobleman.

200

Twenty-five pairs of gladiators fight at the funeral of a wealthy Roman.

146

Rome completes its conquest of Greece and now controls most of the Mediterranean world.

73

A group of inmates at a private gladiator school near the Italian town of Capua escape; one of their number, Spartacus, leads them in a spirited but ultimately futile rebellion against Rome.

65

The Roman politician Julius Caesar presents 320 pairs of gladiators in games he stages in Rome. Hereafter, gladiatorial combats and wild beast shows become increasingly public in character and large in scale.

55

The noted Roman general Gnaeus Pompeius sponsors a wild beast show in which many elephants are pitilessly slaughtered.

31

In the last of several devastating civil wars, Octavian, Caesar's adopted son, defeats his last rivals at Actium (in western Greece). Soon afterward, Octavian is renamed Augustus ("the Revered One") and establishes an autocratic state that comes to be known as the Roman Empire.

A.D.

14

Augustus dies after a long and fruitful reign. By this time, imperial gladiator schools exist across the Empire, and the state has a virtual monopoly on presenting the public games.

30

Skits based on the capture and punishment of a famous brigand named Laureolus begin to be staged in the animal shows.

37–41

The reign of Caligula (Gaius Caesar), the first emperor to fight in the arena like a gladiator.

51–68

The reign of the tyrant Nero, who fights a lion (which has been trained not to attack people) in the arena.

79

The volcano Mount Vesuvius erupts, burying the town of Pompeii. Its amphitheater, gladiator barracks, and many inscriptions mentioning the arena fighters are preserved under the ash for future generations to find and learn from.

80

The emperor Titus inaugurates Rome's new amphitheater, the Colosseum, with games in which some nine thousand animals are slaughtered.

81–96

The reign of Titus's brother, Domitian, who enjoys watching women gladiators.

107

The emperor Trajan stages games in which thousands of gladiators fight and more than eleven thousand beasts are killed.

180–192

The reign of Commodus, who is credited with hundreds of appearances in the arena as either a gladiator or an animal hunter.

193–211

The reign of the emperor Septimius Severus, who bans women from appearing as gladiators.

393

The Christian emperor Theodosius I bans all pagan (non-Christian) religions, possibly ending the Olympic and other Greek festivals featuring athletic competitions. Soon afterward, the gladiator schools are shut down.

430

The approximate date for the last gladiatorial combats in Rome.

476

In the wake of repeated invasions by northern European peoples, the last western Roman emperor is forced from his throne.

FOR FURTHER READING

BOOKS

Lionel Casson, *Daily Life in Ancient Rome.* New York: American Heritage, 1975. A well-written presentation of how the Romans lived: their homes, streets, entertainment, foods, religion, and more.

John Malam, *Secret Worlds: Gladiators.* London: Dorling Kindersley, 2002. A beautifully illustrated book that brings the exciting but bloody gladiatorial combats of ancient Rome to life.

Anthony Marks and Graham Tingay, *The Romans.* London: Usborne, 1990. For basic readers, an excellent summary of the main aspects of Roman history, life, and arts, supported by hundreds of color drawings.

Don Nardo, *Roman Amphitheaters.* New York: Franklin Watts, 2002. Tells about the origins of the stone arenas where gladiators and animal hunters fought and often died, and how these structures were built.

Judith Simpson, *Ancient Rome.* New York: Time-Life, 1997. A beautifully illustrated volume about ancient Roman civilization.

Richard Watkins, *Gladiator.* Boston: Houghton Mifflin, 1997. A very well-written, nicely illustrated overview of gladiators and their world for young readers.

INTERNET SOURCES

Ludus Gladiatorius (www.ludus.org. uk). Presented by an English reenactor group, this site has many links to information about gladiatorial bouts, costumes, weapons, and tactics.

Barbara F. McManus, "Arena: Gladiatorial Games," VRoma. www.vroma. org. An accurate and informative overview of the Roman *munera.*

———, "The Circuses: Roman Chariot Racing," VRoma. www.vroma.org. A well-written general overview of another popular part of the Roman games, chariot racing.

WORKS CONSULTED

MAJOR WORKS

Roland Auguet, *Cruelty and Civilization: The Roman Games.* London: Routledge, 1994. A commendable overview of Roman games, including gladiatorial combats.

Alan Baker, *The Gladiator: The Secret History of Rome's Warrior Slaves.* New York: St. Martin's, 2000. An excellent general discussion of Roman gladiators, including the political and social dimensions of their combats as well as the kinds of fighters and how they fought.

J.P.V.D. Balsdon, *Life and Leisure in Ancient Rome.* New York: McGraw-Hill, 1969. A huge, detailed, and masterful volume on many aspects of Roman life and customs by a highly respected historian.

Carlin A. Barton, *The Sorrow of the Ancient Romans: The Gladiator and the Monster.* Princeton, NJ: Princeton University Press, 1993. A scholarly study of the Roman fascination for gladiators as well as the psychology of the fighters themselves.

Richard C. Beacham, *Spectacle Entertainments of Early Imperial Rome.* New Haven, CT: Yale University Press, 1999. This fine study of the famous Roman games is highlighted by first-class scholarship and an excellent bibliography.

Michael Grant, *Gladiators.* New York: Delacorte, 1967. A brief but comprehensive and readable general study of the subject.

Eckart Kohne, ed., *Gladiators and Caesars: The Power of Spectacle in Ancient Rome.* Berkeley and Los Angeles: University of California Press, 2000. An in-depth, insightful, very well-written treatment of Roman gladiators.

Donald G. Kyle, *Spectacles of Death in Ancient Rome.* New York: Routledge, 2001. An excellent study of gladiators that places special emphasis on the disposal of their remains.

OTHER IMPORTANT WORKS

Ancient Sources in Translation

Ammianus Marcellinus, *History,* published as *The Later Roman Empire, A.D. 354–378.* Trans. and ed. Walter Hamilton. New York: Penguin, 1986.

Augustan History, published as *Lives of the Later Caesars, the First Part of the* Augustan History, *with Newly Compiled Lives of Nerva and Trajan.* Trans. Anthony Birley. New York: Penguin, 1976.

Aulus Gellius, *Attic Nights.* Trans. J.C. Rolfe. 3 vols. Cambridge, MA: Harvard University Press, 1954.

Juvenal, *Satires,* published as *Juvenal: The Sixteen Satires.* Trans. Peter Green. New York: Penguin, 1974.

Livy, *The History of Rome from Its Foundation,* excerpted in *Livy, Vol. 2.* Trans. Canon Roberts. New York: E.P. Dutton, 1912.

Martial, *Epigrams.* 3 vols. Ed. and trans. D.R. Shackleton Bailey. Cambridge, MA: Harvard University Press, 1993.

Petronius, *The Satyricon.* Trans. J.P. Sullivan. New York: Penguin Books, 1977.

Pliny the Elder, *Natural History,* excerpted in *Pliny the Elder: Natural History: A Selection.* Trans. John H. Healy. New York: Penguin, 1991.

Plutarch, *Parallel Lives,* excerpted in *Fall of the Roman Republic: Six Lives by Plutarch.* Trans. Rex Warner. New York: Penguin Books, 1972.

Seneca, *Moral Letters.* Trans. Richard M. Gummere. London: William Heinemann, 1918; *On Benefits.* Trans. Aubrey Stewart. London: George Bell, 1887; and assorted works in *The Stoic Philosophy of Seneca.* Ed. and trans. Moses Hadas. New York: W.W. Norton, 1958.

Jo-Ann Shelton, ed., *As the Romans Did: A Sourcebook in Roman Social History.* New York: Oxford University Press, 1988.

Suetonius, *Lives of the Twelve Caesars,* published as *The Twelve Caesars.* Trans. Robert Graves, rev. Michael Grant. New York: Penguin, 1979.

Tacitus, *The Annals,* published as *The Annals of Ancient Rome.* Trans. Michael Grant. New York: Penguin, 1989.

Modern Sources

Lesley Adkins and Roy A. Adkins, *Handbook to Life in Ancient Rome.* New York: Facts On File, 1994.

Graham Ashford, "The Classic Stance," Ludus Gladiatorius, 2002. www.ludus.org.uk.

———, *"Provocator,"* Ludus Gladiatorius, 2001. www.ludus.org.uk.

———, "Women Gladiators?" Ludus Gladiatorius, 2001. www.ludus.org.uk.

Jerome Carcopino, *Daily Life in Ancient Rome: The People and the City at the Height of the Empire.* Rev. ed. New Haven, CT: Yale University Press, 1992.

Kathleen Coleman, "The Virtues of Violence: Gladiators, the Arena, and the Roman System of Values," a lecture delivered March 26, 2001, at the College of the Holy Cross, Worcester, MA.

Alison Futrell, *Blood in the Arena: The Spectacle of Roman Power.* Austin: University of Texas Press, 1998.

Jean-Claude Golvin, *Amphitheaters and Gladiators.* Paris: CNRS, 1990.

Vera Olivova, *Sport and Games in the Ancient World.* New York: St. Martin's, 1984.

Michael B. Poliakoff, *Combat Sports in the Ancient World.* New Haven, CT: Yale University Press, 1987.

Peter Quennell, *The Colosseum.* New York: Newsweek Book Division, 1971.

Thomas E.J. Wiedemann, *Emperors and Gladiators.* London: Routledge, 1992.

Stephen Wisdom, *Gladiators: 100 B.C.– A.D. 200.* Oxford, UK: Osprey, 2001.

PICTURE CREDITS

ABOUT THE AUTHOR

Historian Don Nardo has published many volumes about ancient Roman history and culture, including *The Punic Wars, The Age of Augustus, A Travel Guide to Ancient Rome, Life of a Roman Slave, The Greenhaven Encyclopedia of Greek and Roman Mythology,* and biographies of Julius Caesar and Cleopatra. Mr. Nardo also writes screenplays and teleplays and composes music. He lives in Massachusetts with his wife, Christine.